The Hidden Treasure
of Black ASL

The Hidden Treasure of Black ASL:

Its History and Structure

Carolyn McCaskill
Ceil Lucas
Robert Bayley
Joseph Hill

In Collaboration With
Roxanne King
Pamela Baldwin
Randall Hogue

GALLAUDET UNIVERSITY PRESS / WASHINGTON, D.C.

Gallaudet University Press
Washington, DC 20002
http://gupress.gallaudet.edu

Library of Congress Cataloging-in-Publication Data

The hidden treasure of Black ASL: its history and structure/Carolyn McCaskill ...
[et al.]; in collaboration with Roxanne King Pamela Baldwin Randall Hogue.
     p.   cm.
  Includes bibliographical references and index.
  ISBN-13: 978-1-56368-489-0 (hard cover: alk. paper)
  ISBN-10: 1-56368-489-6 (hard cover: alk. paper)
  1. American Sign Language. 2. African Americans. 3. Deaf—United States.
I. McCaskill, Carolyn.
HV2545.H53   2011
419'.707—dc22

                                                              2010052968

There's beauty in the way a hand
   Can carve a word on the air,
There's beauty in the way a hand
   Can give lift to a prayer.
There's beauty in the way a hand
   Can trace a song in space,
There's beauty in the way a hand
   Can light a deaf child's face.
Though we can't hear the spoken word
   Or leaves rustling on a tree,
We can hear the beauty
   Of a word that we can see.

—Linwood Smith, "The Way of a Hand"

Contents

Illustrations

Tables

Tables

Foreword

In January 2005 I had the pleasure of serving on Carolyn McCaskill's doctoral dissertation committee at Gallaudet University. At the conclusion of what had been a successful dissertation defense and amid much cheering and hugging, by happenstance I observed a brief conversation between Carolyn and Ceil Lucas, a professor of linguistics at Gallaudet University. In essence, Ceil said, "Let's do research and write a book together." For those who know Ceil, she means what she says. Ceil had a vision and Carolyn had passion. The outcome was the formation of a marvelous partnership that has evolved into the publication of a book and companion DVD titled *The Hidden Treasure of Black ASL: Its History and Structure*.

The book and companion DVD are organized around four guiding questions: (1) What was the sociohistorical reality that would make a separate variety of ASL possible? (2) What are the features of the variety of ASL that people call Black ASL? (3) Can the same kinds of features that have been identified for African American English be identified for Black ASL to show that it is a distinct variety of ASL? and (4) If unique features exist, what are they, and what are the linguistic and social factors that condition their use? The answers to these questions should, at least in part, shed light on an observation made by Hairston and Smith (1983) that "there is . . . a Black way of signing used by Black deaf people in their own cultural milieu—among families and friends, in social gatherings, and in deaf clubs"(55).

The Hidden Treasure of Black ASL is the first and most comprehensive study of Black ASL undertaken since Bill Stokoe's colleague Carl Croneberg stated nearly fifty years ago that "a study of ASL dialects of the Negro deaf will constitute an important part of the full-scale sign language dialect study" (1965, 315). I enthusiastically welcome *The Hidden Treasure of Black ASL* because it paves the way for a deeper understanding and appreciation of what many in both the Black and White Deaf communities have talked about anecdotally as "a Black way of signing used by Black deaf people in their own cultural milieu." The book and companion DVD also offer a conceptual framework and road map to help inspire and foster further research and scholarship on Black ASL.

This book also includes a rich collection of stories about life in segregated schools for Black deaf students and about initial encounters with White teachers and students when the Black and White schools integrated. Readers will especially enjoy the variety of interviews interspersed throughout the DVD, including that with Mary Herring Wright, author of the book *Sounds Like Home: Growing up Black and Deaf in the South* and an alumna of the North Carolina State School for the Blind and Deaf in Raleigh. Wright attended school during the Great Depression and the WW II era.

The chapter on the history of Black deaf schools and the sociohistorical reality that contributed to the transmission of Black ASL from one generation to another, particularly in the South, is one of the most fully developed and well-documented reports published to date. The authors provide valuable insight into how it was possible for a Black variety of ASL—separate from that used in the White Deaf community—to evolve and be passed on from one community of Black deaf users to another over multiple generations. Furthermore, I was especially heartened to learn about the linguistic differences between Black and White ASL. The authors did not find evidence that the ASL used by White signers was better or more advanced than Black ASL. What they did note was, at least in part perhaps as a result of the maintenance of segregated schools throughout much of the twentieth century, that Black ASL had not undergone processes of change such as those that occurred with the variety of ASL used in the White Deaf community. Perhaps Black ASL could be considered akin to a more orthodox or traditional variety of ASL. I also suspect that their findings have the potential to help dispel a common misperception of Black ASL. Their findings challenge members of both Black and White Deaf communities to reassess and reconsider how they perceive and talk about Black ASL. Moreover, how one perceives and talks about Black ASL also has potentially significant implications for the teaching of sociolinguistic variation in ASL courses and for the training of professional personnel such as interpreters and teachers of deaf students.

The Hidden Treasure of Black ASL is a product of an outstanding, as well as unique, collaborative effort among a diverse group of people. It involved a partnership between two academic departments at Gallaudet University—the Department of ASL and Deaf Studies and the Department of Linguistics—and the Department of Linguistics at the University of California at Davis. The research team, which comprised Drs. Carolyn McCaskill, Ceil Lucas, and Robert Bayley, along with Gallaudet University graduate students Joseph Hill (doctoral student in the Department of Linguistics) and Roxanne King (2008 graduate of the MA degree program in ASL and Deaf Studies), and community representative Pamela Baldwin, brought a powerful synergy of scholarly expertise, as well as diverse multicultural and multilingual perspectives, to the project. Additionally, both Carolyn McCaskill and Pamela Baldwin brought first-hand personal experiences to the project as alumnae of segregated schools for the deaf in the South and later as members of the first group of Black students to attend integrated classes on White deaf campuses (Alabama and Arkansas, respectively).

The success of this collaborative effort also involved reaching out to and developing partnerships with target groups of deaf people who, for the most part, have been historically underrepresented in research involving the American Deaf community. The large and diverse number of Black deaf individuals who participated in the research project through interviews and free conversation was remarkable. They reflected a microcosm of the Black Deaf community on the basis of educational attainment, socioeconomic status, type of school attended (segregated, integrated, or a combination of both), use of Black ASL, and a host of other factors. Not only did the team members reach out to the Black Deaf community to develop partnerships for the purposes of collecting data for the project, but they also devoted significant time sharing their results with numerous audiences. These included informal social gatherings such as cookouts for and reunions of former students, as well as formal gatherings such as national and regional conferences of the Black Deaf Advocates and the national conference of Deaf People of Color.

Though Carl Croneberg made his observations nearly fifty years ago about the need for research on "a Black way of signing used by Black deaf people in their own cultural milieu," I believe if he has an opportunity to review *The Hidden Treasure of Black ASL,* he will be pleased. In fact, I think he would more than likely grin from ear to ear and sign, "Job well done!" I, too, heartily applaud the tireless efforts of the research team that authored this treasure of a book.

Glenn B. Anderson, PhD
Department of Counseling, Adult and Rehabilitation Education
University of Arkansas at Little Rock
Former Chair, Gallaudet University Board of Trustees (1994–2005)

REFERENCES

Croneberg, C. G. 1965. Sign Language Dialects. In *A Dictionary of American Sign Language on Linguistic Principles,* ed. W. C. Stokoe Jr., D. C. Casterline, and C. G. Croneberg, 313–19. Washington, D.C.: Gallaudet College Press.

Hairston, E., and L. Smith. 1983. *Black and Deaf in America: Are We That Different?* Silver Spring, Md.: TJ Publishers.

Wright, M. 1999. *Sounds Like Home: Growing up Black and Deaf in the South.* Washington, D.C.: Gallaudet University Press.

Acknowledgments

A project such as the one represented in this book and its accompanying DVD cannot be completed without the assistance and input of many people. First, we gratefully acknowledge the people at each of the six sites who participated in the filming and helped us with the arrangements and photos. They are as follows: in North Carolina, Lawrence Carter, Daisy Rivenbark, Barbara Crockett-Dease, Linda Carr, and Reginald Redding in Louisiana, Anthony Aramburo, Ester McAllister; at Southern University and A&M College, Emma Perry, Angela Proctor, and Edward Pratt; in Alabama, Patrick Robinson, Evon Black, Terry Graham, and Pam Shaw; in Arkansas, Barbara Mangum Harrison; in Texas, Essie Smith, Terold Gallien, and Betty Henderson; and in Virginia, Dorothy West and Donna Stone; and at Hampton University, Yuri Milligan.

We also acknowledge our colleagues at Gallaudet University: in Video Services, Paul Filiatreault, Ron Reed, Patrick Harris, Gary Brooks, Barry White, Rosemary Bennett, and Earl Parks; in the Gallaudet University Archives, Ulf Hedberg, Mike Olson, and Jeff Peterson; at Gallaudet University Press, Ivey Wallace, Dan Wallace, Deirdre Mullervy, Carol Hoke, Frances Clark, Valencia Simmons, and Donna Thomas.

Other Gallaudet colleagues and our colleagues "at large" provided valuable support and insight at various points—Jean Bergey of the *History through Deaf Eyes Project,* Todd Byrd of *On the Green,* Christine Katsapis and Audrey Foster of the Office of Sponsored Programs, Jayne McKenzie, Lindsay Dunn, Joseph Murray, Brian Greenwald, Bill Marshall, Donna Mertens, Jane Dillehay, Roz Rosen, Jane K. Fernandes, Karen Kimmel, Isaac Agboola, Ernie Hairston, Glenn Anderson, Nathie Marbury, Gary Wait, Allan Metcalf, Ed Finegan, Walt Wolfram, Greg Guy, John Rickford, Haj Ross, Patricia Cukor-Avila, John Baugh, Joan Maling, Trevor Johnston, Claudia Copeland, the Department of ASL and Deaf Studies and the

Department of Linguistics at Gallaudet University; the Department of Linguistics at the University of California at Davis; National Black Deaf Advocates and especially Ernest Garrett III, Benro Ogunyipe, and Bola Desalu; our research assistants Anika Stephen, Stephanie Johnson, TaWanda Barkely, and Page Roberts, as well as the folks at ParsIntl: Jennifer Freeman, Yan Wu, and Monique Parish.

This book and DVD are based on work supported by the Spencer Foundation and by the National Science Foundation under grants BCS-0813736 and DRL-0936085. We are very grateful for this support. Finally, we are indebted to our significant others and friends who provided cheerful and unwavering support throughout the project: Janie McCaskill, Jacqueline McCaskill, Angela McCaskill, Sharrell McCaskill, Darrell McCaskill, Jamel McCaskill, Deron Emerson, Doris Shoots, Stephen Brown, Franklin and Kathleen Brown, Ann Robinson, Etta Hill, Alesia Howard Allen, Argiroula Zangana, Beverly Kamara, Royale Loibman, David King, and Amina King.

1

Introduction

Without a doubt, the question asked most frequently by laypersons as they turn their attention to sign languages and Deaf communities is whether sign language is universal (i.e., whether only one sign language is known and used by Deaf people all over the world).[1] The answer, which is most often greeted with surprise, is that there is no universal sign language in the sense that the questioner intends it. There have been attempts to devise and implement systems that can be understood by deaf people in situations such as international conferences (Rosenstock 2003), with decidedly mixed results. However, there is no one naturally occurring universal sign language to which all deaf people somehow have access. There are basically as many sign languages as there are viable Deaf communities, as well as sign languages that exist alongside the spoken languages of the majority communities. These sign languages are also differentiated internally according to social criteria in the same way that spoken languages are. That is, varieties of sign languages exist, and the social factors that help define them include both those that play a role in spoken-language variation—region, age, gender, socioeconomic status, race—and others that are unique to language use in Deaf communities. The latter include the language policies implemented in deaf education, the home environment (e.g., Deaf parents in an ASL-signing home vs. hearing parents in a nonsigning home) and the sightedness [or not] of the signer, as in Tactile ASL, the variety used by deaf-blind individuals.

---

1. The use of uppercase "Deaf" here indicates cultural deafness, as opposed to the strictly audiological condition indicated by lowercase "deaf." Both uses are conventional in the literature on deafness.

This book and its accompanying DVD describe a project about one such variety of American Sign Language (ASL) used by African American signers and usually known as Black ASL. (The symbol [DVD icon] indicates a link to a relevant section of the DVD.) Hairston and Smith have stated that there is "a Black way of signing used by Black deaf people in their own cultural milieu—among families and friends, in social gatherings, and in deaf clubs" (1983, 55). There is abundant anecdotal evidence that such a variety exists. For example, one of the senior members of the research team, Carolyn McCaskill, talks about "putting my signs aside" when she arrived at the newly integrated Alabama School for the Deaf (ASD) in Talladega in 1968. She had previously attended the segregated Alabama School for Negro Deaf (ASND) and was one of about ten Black deaf students (five females and five males) who transferred to the school. She and the other students found classroom communication very challenging. They were very surprised to find how different the signing was at their new school and how difficult it was at first to understand the White students and the teachers. The teacher asked them, "What are you signing?" and the students asked her the same question. She and the other Black deaf students felt as if they were signing two different languages and in a foreign land. Ironically, the school for Black children and the school for the White children were located within a few miles of each other. As another example, a young hearing man from a Black deaf family (a Coda, 'child of deaf adults') who teaches ASL at a community college remarks, "Oh yeah—the way I sign in class and the way I sign at home are totally different." Black Deaf participants and interpreters attending meetings of the National Black Deaf Advocates (NBDA) have been known to observe, "I see something different—different from other signing." Thus, although we have had only fairly small-scale studies (see, e.g., Aramburo 1989; Guggenheim 1993; Lewis 1998), we do have numerous anecdotal accounts that a distinct dialect exists.

Since William C. Stokoe's (1960) pioneering work, linguists have recognized that natural sign languages are autonomous linguistic systems, structurally independent of the spoken languages with which they may coexist in a given community. This recognition has been followed by extensive research into different aspects of ASL structure and accompanied by the recognition that, as natural sign languages are full-fledged autonomous linguistic systems shared by communities of users, the sociolinguistics of sign languages can be described in ways that parallel the description of the sociolinguistics of spoken languages. On Stokoe's pioneering work, Garretson (1980) remarked that, "To know, once and for all, that our 'primitive' and 'ideographic gestures' are really a formal language on a par with all other languages of the world is a step towards pride and liberation" (vi). A *formal language* by definition includes sociolinguistic variation and distinct subsystems or varieties. As of this writing, we have clear empirical evidence of one such variety of ASL, the Tactile ASL used by deaf-blind signers, which is distinct in its phonology,[2] morphosyntax, lexicon, and discourse structure from "sighted ASL" (Collins and Petronio 1998; Collins 2004). There is a widespread perception in the American Deaf community that Black ASL exists, and (mostly) anecdotal reports indicate that it is as distinct from the ASL used by White signers as vernacular African American English (AAE) is from middle-class White English (as seen earlier). However, empirical studies of Black ASL based on natural language have not previously been conducted. This book and DVD are the first steps to filling that gap in our knowledge. In the following pages, we address four main questions:

1. What sociohistorical reality would make a separate variety of ASL possible?
2. What are the features of the variety of ASL that people call "Black ASL"?[3]

---

2. The term *phonology* is used in sign linguistics to describe the same area of linguistics that it refers to in spoken language studies (i.e., the study of the basic units of the language, in this case handshape, location, palm orientation, movement, and facial expressions).

3. We use the term *variety* throughout to avoid the negative connotations associated with the term *dialect*. As linguists, we are of course aware that we all speak or sign one dialect or another, but in popular usage, the term *dialect* has come to be associated with language varieties that diverge from and are somehow less worthy than a "standard" language.

3. Can the same kinds of unique features that have been identified for African American English be identified for Black ASL to show that it is a distinct variety of ASL?
4. If unique features exist, what are they, and what are the linguistic and social factors that condition their use?

How Language Varieties Come About

In order to describe Black ASL as a distinct variety of ASL, we should examine whether the sociohistorical conditions that Black and White Deaf people have experienced might have led to the emergence of a separate variety. This requires one more step back to ask how language varieties come about in general, whether signed or spoken. In a study of African American English, Rickford states, "All languages, if they have enough speakers, have dialects—regional or social varieties that develop when people are separated by geographic or social barriers" (1999, 320). There are a number of geographic and social factors involved in the formation of language varieties. Wolfram and Schilling-Estes (2006) state that "Dialects are most likely to develop where we find both physical and social separation among groups of speakers" (29). They discuss the factors involved in dialect formation, which include settlement patterns, migration, geographic features, language contact, economic ecology, social stratification, social interaction (e.g., social practices, speech communities), and group and individual identity. Settlement patterns have both to do with where people come from and where they settle. For example, "the initial patterns of habitation by English speakers from various parts of the British Isles, as well as by emigrants and enslaved peoples who spoke languages other than English, are still reflected in the patterning of dialect differentiation in the United States today" (30). Wolfram and Schilling-Estes go on to explain that, once settlements are established, dialect boundaries may reflect migration from these points and that geographic features such as mountains, rivers, and lakes are important insofar as they shape migration routes. Geographic isolation of course plays a role, as Bergmann, Hall, and Ross point out in *Language Files:* "[B]eing isolated from other speakers tends to allow a dialect to develop in its own way, through its own innovations that are different from those of other dialects" (2007, 419). Wolfram and Schilling-Estes further observe: "The most effective kind of communication is face-to-face, and when groups of speakers do not interact on a personal level with one another, the likelihood of dialect divergence is heightened" (2006, 32). Political boundaries such as national or local borders also need to be considered. Contact with other language groups also plays a role in the formation of dialects, as does economic ecology: "Different economic bases not only bring about the development of specialized vocabulary items associated with different occupations; they also may affect the direction and rate of language change in grammar and pronunciation" (34). Socioeconomic status has a well-documented role in the formation of varieties, as do social networks (Milroy 1987) (i.e., with whom people interact and talk on a daily basis).

A very useful construct is that of *communities of practice* (Eckert and McConnell-Ginet 1992; Lave and Wenger 1991). Eckert (2000) defines such a group as "an aggregate of people who come together around some enterprise" and as "simultaneously defined by its membership and the shared practices in which that membership engages" (35). Communities of practice (CofP) are "dynamic and fluid" groups in which individuals "are seen as active agents in the construction of individual and group identity, rather than simply as passive respondents to the social situations in which they find themselves" (Wolfram and Schilling-Estes 2006, 38). The idea of the CofP has often been more helpful in explaining patterns of variation than, say, more rigid notions of social class imposed by the researcher (Bucholtz 1999). Finally, group membership, whether voluntary or coerced, and personal identity have also been seen to have played roles in the emergence of language varieties.

Wolfram and Schilling-Estes (2006) also identify a number of linguistic factors such as rule extension, analogy, grammaticalization, phonological processes (e.g., assimilation), and word-formation processes (i.e., factors in dialect formation having to do specifically with the structure of language). As a result of these social and linguistic factors, we see differences between middle-class and working-class speech, varieties shaped by social class, age, gender, and ethnicity, as in the case of the Spanish used in the Southwest. As Wolfram and Schilling-Estes state, "These linguistic and social factors may come together in a myriad of ways, resulting in a multitude of dialects" (24).

Of course, varieties can also lose some of their distinctive characteristics when users of different dialects come into regular contact with each other. For example, in the United States, dialects on the East Coast tend to reflect the varieties of English brought by the original settlers. In the West, however, these differences became less distinct as settlers from north and south mingled on the frontier. In a similar way, we might expect to see differences between Black and White ASL become less noticeable as a result of the integration of residential schools and the increase in integrated mainstream programs. In several of the following chapters we address the question of whether Black and White ASL are becoming more similar or are maintaining their linguistic distinctiveness.

African American English

African American English[4] (AAE) is a very well-documented variety of English that illustrates the role of these geographic and social factors in the formation of a language variety. It is also directly relevant to the project described in this book. More than fifty years of research findings have documented the structure and use of AAE in rich detail. In addition, AAE has been shown to be a rule-governed and systematic variety of English distinct in its structure from other varieties of English, a variety that acquired its distinctiveness over a long period of time and as a result of the

---

4. The variety of English spoken by African Americans in the rural South and inner cities of the North has been referred to by a number of names, including Black English Vernacular (BEV), African American Vernacular English (AAVE), and, most recently, African American English (AAE), the term we have adopted here. These terms all refer to a distinct dialect that differs in structure and pronunciation from general U.S. English spoken by members of all racial groups, including, of course, many African Americans.

interaction of many historical and social forces.[5] Furthermore, not only linguists but also both Black and White laypersons recognize AAE as distinct from other English varieties. While laypersons and linguists may use different labels to identify this variety (e.g., Ebonics), they nevertheless easily and clearly perceive it to be distinct from middle class White English, as well as from other varieties of English. Moreover, many empirical descriptions of AAE structure and use solidly confirm laypersons' perceptions of distinctiveness.

Another Variety of ASL: Tactile ASL

Research on other varieties of ASL is also relevant to the present volume, most notably the work on what is known as Tactile ASL, the variety of ASL used by deaf-blind people, specifically those with the genetic condition Usher syndrome I. Individuals with this condition are born deaf and later, usually in their teenage years, start losing vision in varying degrees due to retinitis pigmentosa, a hereditary condition that is characterized by progressive loss of peripheral vision and eventually leads to central vision loss. Crucially, most deaf-blind people in this category grow up using ASL and are fluent signers by the time they begin to lose their sight. A variety of ASL has emerged in this community that accommodates the loss of sight at all linguistic levels: phonological, morphological, syntactic, and discourse. One of the consequences of the loss of sight is that deaf-blind people no longer have access to the numerous ASL grammatical and discourse markers produced on a signer's face. Remarkably, these non-manual (facial) markers are produced on the hands in Tactile ASL. For example, the raised eyebrows required for yes/no questions or the nodding required for back-channeling are produced manually (see Collins and

---

5. See Mufwene et al. (1998) and Green (2004) for reviews of the AAE literature. Edwards (2008) and Wolfram (2008) provide succinct outlines of the main distinctive features of AAE phonology and grammar, while Green (2002) provides a detailed analysis of AAE linguistic structure. Rickford and Rickford (2000) offer a nontechnical discussion of AAE and its place in African American life and culture.

Petronio 1998 and Collins 2004 for fuller accounts). As mentioned, features of Tactile ASL appear at every level of the language, and there is a vigorous community of deaf-blind signers who use Tactile ASL. Tactile ASL qualifies as a clear example of a variety of ASL. In addition, research has demonstrated the existence of tactile varieties of other sign languages such as Swedish Sign Language (Mesch 2000) and Norwegian Sign Language (Raanes 2006). The project we describe here explores the specific linguistic and sociolinguistic factors that might qualify Black ASL as a variety of ASL in the same way that Tactile ASL has been shown to be a variety of ASL. People say, "I see something different—different from other signing," and it is our goal to describe what that "something" is and which factors have contributed to its formation.

So What About Black ASL?

We return now to the physical and social factors that Wolfram and Schilling-Estes (2006) describe as playing a role in shaping language varieties. As for settlement patterns, migration, and geographic isolation, the physical and social segregation and oppression that have affected the Black hearing community and contributed to the emergence of AAE have also affected the Black Deaf community. In the chapter on race, deafness, and ASL in his book on the history of ASL, Tabak (2006) lists physical isolation and geography as two of three factors that "have served to increase the variability of American Sign Language among African-American Deaf" (98).[6] The reality that unites physical and social segregation and oppression is the establishment of separate schools or departments for Black deaf children. As chapter 2 explains, such schools and departments were established in seventeen states and in the District of Columbia.

Until well after the Supreme Court's 1954 ruling in *Brown vs. Board of Education,* which made segregation illegal, Black children's contact

---

6. The third factor that Tabak lists is the existence of temporal variation in any language, such that older Black Deaf signers sign differently from younger ones. That is, like all living languages and dialects, Black ASL changes over time.

with White people was for the most part limited to the school context. This is quite different from the integrated school environments that the younger signers in our study experienced. However, as chapter 4 explains, younger and older signers alike show a clear sense of group reference and personal identity as "Black Deaf" and can explain differences between Black signing and White signing. As Wolfram and Schilling-Estes state, "Sometimes, group membership is voluntary and negotiated by the individual and the various groups to which they seek to belong, and sometimes it is rooted in established social strictures (e.g., class or gender groups) and is not completely a matter of choice—or at least [a] very easy choice" (2006, 41). Attendance by Black deaf children at segregated schools or departments was clearly a matter of discrimination and racism and never a matter of choice, but the result was a strong sense of group membership and personal identity.

As for linguistic explanations of the existence of language varieties, in chapters 5, 6, and 7 we explore specific features pertaining to phonological variation, variation in syntax and discourse, and the outcomes of language contact, specifically that between ASL and AAE. Chapter 8 focuses on the lexical variation in our data, both as produced by the signers who participated and as they discussed it. We are, of course, aware of an abundance of lexical differences between Black and White signers, and we account for those in our data. However, our goal is to take the analysis beyond lexical variation to other linguistic features such as handedness (i.e., use of two-handed signs or their corresponding one-handed variants), the size of the signing space, the lowering of signs (for example, from the forehead to the face or the space in front of the signer), and the use of voiceless mouthing, clausal repetition, constructed action, and constructed dialogue, as well as the incorporation of AAE into the signing. What we propose is a mosaic of features.

Figure 1.1 shows eight features that may serve to differentiate Black ASL from the ASL used by White signers. Six of the features (all except for lexical differences and the incorporation of AAE into the signing) are features of the ASL used by White signers, so what we are talking about is not a qualitative difference between Black signers and White signers

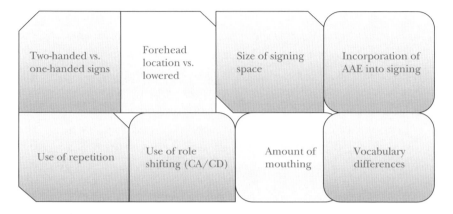

Figure 1.1. Possible distinguishing features of Black ASL.

but rather a quantitative one—that is, all ASL signers use these features, but Black signers may use them to a greater or lesser degree. When someone says, "Yeah, I see something different," what they may be seeing is some combination of these eight features. According to Tabak (2006), "Nor can one point to a particular linguistic idiosyncrasy that is unique to the signed language of African-Americans—at least not in the sense that there exists a phrase or a grammatical convention that is shared by all African-American Deaf and no others" (98), and, in terms of six of the features in the mosaic, he is correct. However, his remark is evidently based entirely on his own personal observations since he does not report on any empirical data as a basis for this remark. His remark also overlooks a significant amount of lexical variation that distinguishes Black ASL from other varieties, as well as the incorporation of AAE features into Black ASL, something that, while it may subsequently be borrowed by White signers, clearly originates with Black signers. Furthermore, as we will see, the difference between Black signers and White signers in the use of repetition is quite striking, making it something that is almost unique to Black signers. Interestingly, Tabak does list lexical variation—"some differences in vocabulary"—as well as the size of the signing space and voiceless mouthing as differences between the students at the school for Black deaf children in Texas and the school for White deaf students. The size of the signing space and voiceless mouthing are two of the features in our mosaic. Again, Tabak's remarks here seem to be based entirely on his own observation, as no source of data is reported. Burch and Joyner (2007) also report descriptions from two interviewees who commented on the signing at the Raleigh school. Although the interviewees referred to major differences between "Raleigh signs and ASL," Burch and Joyner do not provide any examples.

Earlier Research

Research on all aspects of the structure and use of ASL and other sign languages has progressed continuously since Stokoe's work in the 1960s (see Brentari 2010 and Emmorey and Lane 2000 for overviews). Researchers have also noticed differences between Black and White signing for at least forty years. Linguistic descriptions of the differences between Black and White signing focus primarily on Black signers in the South. For example, in his appendices to the 1965 *Dictionary of American Sign Language* (DASL), which he coauthored with William Stokoe and Dorothy Casterline, Croneberg discusses these differences as a consequence of the segregation of deaf schools in the South. Based on responses to a 134-item sign vocabulary list, he reports "a radical dialect difference between the signs" of a young North Carolina Black woman and those of White signers living in the same city (315). Other studies of Black ASL, which are described in detail in the chapters dealing with specific linguistic features, are mostly small scale. They include work on phonology (Lucas, Bayley, and Valli 2001; Woodward, Erting, and Oliver 1996; Woodward and DeSantis 1977), lexical variation (Aramburo 1989; Guggenheim 1993; Lucas, Bayley, Reed, and Wulf 2001), language attitudes (Lewis, Palmer, and Williams 1995), and parallels between Black ASL and African American speech styles (Lewis 1998).

The role of deaf education in the development of ASL varieties has also been a subject of investigation. Lucas, Bayley, and Valli (2001) showed a clear and strong link between linguistic variation in ASL and the history of deaf education, in particular the language policies implemented at schools for the deaf over the years. These policies ranged from the use of ASL in the classroom beginning in 1817 at the first school, the American School for the Deaf in Hartford, Connecticut, through the strict oralism that was enforced in most schools from the 1880s through the early 1970s (to the exclusion of sign language in the classroom), to the various "combined" methods of signing and talking simultaneously implemented in the 1970s, and finally back to the use of ASL in the classroom in many schools today. The signers who participated in the research of Lucas, Bayley, and Valli (2001) were divided into three age groups according to the language policy in place at the time they were in school: 55 and older (oralist), 26–54 (combined method, and also the period when Stokoe was beginning his research and ASL was starting to be recognized as a real language), and 15–25 (in the project sites, which used ASL as the medium of instruction in the classroom). This division proved to be statistically significant for all of the phonological and the syntactic variables examined.

Much of the prior work on Black ASL was undertaken some years ago. Most of the more recent work has focused on the signing of single individuals or small groups, often in interview situations, which may influence how the participants sign. While building on these earlier studies, the project described in this book provides a more comprehensive description of Black ASL based on a broader sampling of southern Black Deaf communities. By including a broad sample of Black men and women of different ages who live in a range of communities, this volume documents an important aspect of Deaf culture and illustrates a little-studied aspect of the African American experience.

To answer our research questions and to provide a full account of the history and structure of Black ASL, we have taken three major areas into account, as seen in figure 1.2.

We looked, of course, at the sociohistorical foundation: the history of education for Black deaf children and the social conditions that would make the emergence of a variety of ASL possible. We also conducted basic sociolinguistic analyses of eight specific linguistic features to understand what the variety looks like structurally. However, we also took into account our participants' perceptions of education and language. We found a number of recurring themes emerging both from the free conversations

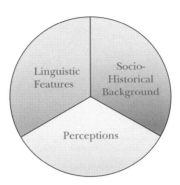

Figure 1.2. Main topics addressed in this study.

and the interviews. The picture would not be complete without these, as they relate directly to the sociohistorical foundation; in addition, their perceptions are both similar to and different from the linguistic findings.

Finally, a word about the title of this book and the DVD, *The Hidden Treasure of Black ASL*. When we started the project, we knew that it would be interesting, but we did not realize how very rich all aspects of it would be—the history of education for Black deaf children in the United States, the perceptions and memories of community members, and the results of our linguistic analyses. We were constantly amazed at what we found, and we realized that this is a story that has not yet received a full telling by any means. We often felt that we were discovering hidden treasures. This is what we offer now, with the strong hope that others will want to continue exploring all aspects of this story.

The Sociohistorical Foundation of Black ASL

In chapter 1 we saw the factors that come into play in the formation of language varieties. In this chapter we examine the history of deaf education for both Black and White children in the United States, with emphasis on deaf education in the South. We begin with an overview of the education of White deaf children, which started in 1817 in Hartford, Connecticut. The education of Black deaf children did not begin until approximately fifty years later. We examine how *Brown v. Board of Education* not only impacted public schooling in general but also played a pivotal role in the desegregation of the schools for deaf children. We analyze the language used and discuss what kind of language the children brought to school. In addition, we discuss the roles of African American and White hearing and Deaf teachers in the education of the participants in the current study. Finally, we outline the history of the six sites where we collected data for our study.

GEOGRAPHICAL AND SOCIAL ISOLATION

As we saw in chapter 1, geographical and social factors played an important role in the formation of the Black deaf schools and consequently in the development of a separate variety of ASL. The geographic factors include the isolation of one community from another; geographic and political boundaries (i.e., where people live—or are allowed to live). Schools for Black deaf children certainly met these conditions. They were often physically isolated. Separate schools, as well as so-called Colored Departments of White schools, were established in southern and border states. Sometimes, the "Colored Department" was on the same campus as the White school (e.g., in Kansas and Missouri), but in other states, these departments were physically separated (e.g., in Georgia and Mississippi) (Baynton 1996).

SOCIAL FACTORS

The same geographic and social factors that promote the formation of spoken language varieties also surround the formation of Black ASL. Not surprisingly, Black deaf people were affected both by the same racial discrimination of the era that affected Black hearing people and by the same social isolation and marginalization due to race that contributed to the development and maintenance of African American English (AAE). Racial discrimination was present in local, state, and regional organizations in the Deaf community. The National Association of the Deaf (NAD) was founded in 1880. At first the association welcomed Black Deaf Americans. However, in 1925, the Cleveland Conference of the NAD revoked the membership of the Black members, changing the bylaws to prohibit Black Deaf membership (Burch 2002; Tabak 2006). Black people (and women) had to wait until 1964 to gain the right to vote in the association (Burch 2002).

Guggenheim (1993) suggests that the separation of Deaf African Americans and European Americans was likely due, in part, to segregated schooling and the consequent development of language differences. Paul C. Higgins (1987) explains, "Different signs developed in the segregated school settings" (52). Studies of Black people in the Chicago and Washington, D.C., Deaf communities in the 1980s reported that clubs and congregations were still segregated and that the races rarely intermingled (Aramburo 1989; Higgins 1987).

Black deaf children were impacted in particular ways; for example, some states had laws requiring that Black deaf students be taught only by Black teachers (Doctor 1948). Tennessee, for example, passed such a law in March 1901 (*History of the Negro Department at the Tennessee School for the Deaf* 1945; Gannon 1981).

THE HISTORY OF DEAF EDUCATION

The publicly supported education of White deaf Americans began in 1817 in Hartford, Connecticut, with the establishment of the Connecticut Asylum for the Education and Instruction of Deaf and Dumb Persons, later renamed the American School for the Deaf (ASD) (van Cleve and Crouch 1989). In 1825, ASD admitted Black deaf students and became the first integrated school in Connecticut (Wait 2008). Figure 2.1 shows a cooking class at ASD in 1906–1907.

Following the founding of ASD, more schools were established in northern states such as New York, Pennsylvania, and Ohio (Moores 1987), and these schools had small Black populations. However, some Black deaf students were educated in northern schools and classes for the deaf (Brill 1950).

Racial segregation in its modern form began in the late 1800s. Slavery, which had existed in the United States for more than two hundred years

Figure 2.1. A cooking class at the American School for the Deaf in Hartford, Connecticut (1906–1907). (Photograph courtesy of the American School for the Deaf. Used by permission.)

prior to the Civil War, resulted in a public policy in the South that prohib-ited the education of Blacks. It was illegal during that era to teach Blacks, whether slave or free, to read or write because the White power structure feared the potential influence of educated Black people. In addition, if Black people were educated, claims of inferiority would be harder to main-tain. Those discovered learning to read or write were frequently severely punished (Boyd-Franklin and Franklin 2000).

Schools for the deaf belatedly reflected the changing attitudes in American society. Additional attempts were made to provide education for Black deaf children. In 1856 Dr. Platt H. Skinner established the P. H. Skinner School for the Deaf, Dumb, and Blind in Niagara Falls, New York. Although Skinner's background was controversial, he is still considered a pioneer. He is probably the first educator to attempt to pro-vide formal education for Black deaf students. He was also an abolitionist who taught fugitives and free slaves to read and write. Skinner wrote the following:

> We are aware that it is a novel thing—that [it] is the first effort of its kind in the country: but why not these poor unfortunate despised African children become useful independent and happy citizens? Why not they be producers instead of consum-ers? Why not they inhabit pleasant and cheerful homes of their own, instead of our poorhouses, jails, and penitentiaries, or sit upon the corners of our streets and beg? We receive and instruct those and those only who are refused admission to all other institutions, and are despised on account of their color. (Skinner 1859, 117)

The School for Colored Deaf, Dumb, and Blind moved to Trenton, New Jersey, in 1860 and closed in 1866 (Dunn 1995; Fay 1893).

After the Civil War, schools for Black deaf children slowly began to emerge. A large number of states established "separate but equal" residen-tial schools for Black deaf students (Fay 1893; Gannon 1981). In the North, no separate schools for Blacks were established, but Baynton (1996) has reported that the Clarke School in Northampton, Massachusetts, which favored oral instruction, in 1908 affirmed a policy of excluding Black students. However, some states did allow Black deaf students to attend classes with their White deaf counterparts.

Legal Challenges to Segregation

The first challenge to the segregation of Black and White deaf children began in 1951. In *Miller v. Board of Education of the District of Columbia*, Mrs. Louise Miller, the mother of a Black deaf child, sued to overturn the District of Columbia legislation that forced Black deaf children to attend school outside the district, either the Maryland School for the Colored Deaf in Overlea or another school. Unhappy with the conditions and instruction at the Maryland school, the Millers sent their son to the Pennsylvania School for the Deaf in Philadelphia in 1949 (Jowers 2005; White 1990). In 1952 a federal district court ruled that Black deaf children had the right to attend the Kendall School, although they remained in segregated classes there until 1958.

Two years after the Miller case was decided, on May 17, 1954, the U.S. Supreme Court ruled in *Brown v. Board of Education* that "racially segregated schools are inherently unequal" and that segregated schools for Black and White students must be abolished (Frankenberg and Lee 2002). The Court found support for its decision in studies that indicated that minority students learn better in racially mixed classrooms (Willie 1987). According to Frankenberg and Lee, "From the late 1960s on, some districts in all parts of the country began implementing such [desegregation] plans, although the courts made it much more difficult to win desegregation orders outside the South" (2002, 2). Opposition to *Brown* was intense in some southern states. Governor George Wallace of Alabama famously stood in a doorway at the University of Alabama, and angry Whites terrorized Blacks (Finkleman 2002). As we will see, this landmark decision affected not only hearing students but Deaf students also.

THE HISTORY OF BLACK DEAF EDUCATION: BEFORE AND AFTER
BROWN V. BOARD OF EDUCATION

In seventeen southern and border states, Deaf schools followed the patterns of segregation that characterized the public schools. These schools were designed to house both Black deaf and Black blind students. In the 1950s thirteen states were still operating segregated schools for the deaf, and most were located in the South. As late as 1963, eight states still maintained separate facilities (Hairston and Smith 1983).

Table 2.1 shows the states that had Black Deaf schools or departments. The second column shows the year that the White deaf school was established. The third column shows the year that the Black deaf school or department was established, and the fourth column shows the year the schools were desegregated. The fifth and sixth columns show the time between the founding of the White and Black schools and between the founding of Black schools and desegregation. The average number of years between the establishment of the White school and the establishment of the Black school (or department) is 33. In some states, however, the time was considerably longer. Kentucky waited 61 years, West Virginia 56 years, Virginia 70 years, and Louisiana 86 years. The average number of years between the establishment of the Black school (or department) and desegregation is 72.8. The striking exceptions are Washington, D.C., with 101 years, and North Carolina, with 98 years. Note that the time between the establishment of a school for Black children and desegregation in Louisiana totaled only 40 years because there was no school for Black deaf children until 1938, and desegregation did not occur until 24 years after *Brown v Board of Education*. Some states accepted students from other states for educational instruction. For example, Blacks from West Virginia were sent to school in Overlea, Maryland (Jowers 2005). The Louisiana participants in this project explained that formal education was not available to them until 1938. The only options for Blacks were to attend school in Mississippi, to attend public school without support services such as interpreters or note takers in the classroom, or to remain at home.

Table 2.1. Black and White Deaf Schools: Founding and Desegregation

State	White school established	Black school/ department established	Desegregation	Years between establishment of Black and White schools	Years between establishment of Black schools and desegregation
DC, KDES	1857	1857 (dept.)	1958	0	101
N. Carolina	1845	1868–1869	1967	24	98
Maryland	1868	1872	1956	4	84
Tennessee	1845	1881 (dept.)	1965	36	84
Georgia	1846	1882	1965	36	83
Mississippi	1854	1882 (dept.)	1965	28	83
S. Carolina	1849	1883 (dept.)	1966	34	83
Kentucky	1823	1884 (dept.)	1954–60	61	70
Florida	1885	1885	1965	0	80
Texas	1857	1887	1965	30	78
Arkansas	1850/1867	1887	1967	37	80
Alabama	1858	1892	1968	34	76
Missouri	1861	1888 (dept.)	1954	37	66
Kansas	1861	1888, dept	1954	27	66
Virginia	1839	1909	1965 (2 schools)	70	56
Oklahoma	1898	1909, dept	1962	11	53
Louisiana	1852	1938	1978	86	40
W. Virginia	1870	1926	1956	56	30

Note. Adapted from *American Annals of the Deaf* (1951 January); Fay (1893).

Higher education for Black deaf students was also a challenge. Mary Herring Wright, a former student of the North Carolina School for the Colored Deaf and Blind (NCSCDB) recounts that she had heard about a college for the deaf in Washington, but it turned out to be only for Whites. The principal of her school discussed with her mother the possibilities of her attending a local college. In her autobiography, Wright recounts the following conversation with her mother:

> I said he told me how smart and intelligent you are and that he hated to see your education end here. He, Miss Watford, and Mr. Mask all said they'd looked into the possibility of you going to Shaw University next year, but you'd need an interpreter for classroom work. They said the state didn't provide for that and it would be too costly. (Wright 1999, 248)

Wright graduated from the school in 1941. After graduation, she was hired as a teacher at the NCSCDB for one year. The school felt she was an excellent role model for the students. Since she did not have the necessary degree, however, she eventually left the school and moved to Washington, D.C., to work at the U.S. Department of the Navy.

William "Bill" King, a graduate of Indiana State School for the Deaf in Indianapolis, faced a similar predicament. He was excited at the thought of attending Gallaudet College with his classmates. When he was informed that he could not attend Gallaudet because of the color of his skin, he was devastated. King applied to the West Virginia State College, a historically Black college and university (HBCU). After graduation, he was hired as a teacher for deaf students at the West Virginia School for the Colored Deaf in Institute, West Virginia (Vale 1948).

In addition to a number of Black deaf residential schools in the United States, there were several day schools and day classes for Black children enrolled in public schools. As table 2.2 shows, some of these classes were not established until the middle of the twentieth century.

Table 2.2. Day Schools and Day Classes for Black Children

School/Class Location	Year Established
St. Louis, Missouri	1925
Baltimore, Maryland	1938
Kansas City, Missouri	1939
Richmond, Virginia	1939
Shreveport, Louisiana	1950
Louisville, Kentucky	1951

Adapted from *American Annals of the Deaf* (January 1951)

FACTORS THAT AFFECT BLACK DEAF EDUCATION

To understand the development of Black ASL, we need to explore three issues. First, who taught at the Black schools in the South? Were they hearing or deaf, Black or White, and did they have formal training in teaching deaf children? Second, did oralism have the same role in the education of Black deaf children as it did in the education of White deaf children? That is, did Black children receive instruction in signed language, or did they suffer from exclusively oral instruction? Finally, what kind of language did children from Black deaf families bring to school? Was it ASL, a distinct variety of ASL, or a system of homesigns? Unfortunately, information is scarce regarding this last factor, and we only touch on it later.

The Teachers

Historically, African American educators have been the largest group of professionals to provide leadership within the community. Throughout the nineteenth century and the first half of the twentieth, African American educators in African American private and public schools held themselves responsible for the educational achievement of the children and adults attending their schools (Franklin 1990; Neverdon-Morton 1989) and viewed education as the way to achieve individual enrichment, as well as social progress (Weiler 1990).

In the early years of deaf education in the South, there was a mixture of Black and White and deaf and hearing teachers, at least at some schools. In North Carolina, for example, the superintendent from 1896 to 1918 was John E. Ray, a hearing advocate of deaf teachers and sign communication. He hired deaf faculty, both Black and White, including Thomas and David Tillinghast, Blanche Wilkins, and Thomas Flowers. Wilkins and Flowers were both Black and were obvious role models for the students (Burch and Joyner 2007, 20–21).

African American teachers were important for the children they taught because the children needed to see that teachers of color could exist and that people of color could assume leadership positions, as well as serve in many other roles (King 1993). Many scholars have called attention to the need for representative role models for children and youth (e.g., Adair 1984; Graham 1987; Stewart et al. 1989). Historically, the low academic achievement of minority students has been attributed in part to the minimal presence of minority professionals in public education (Andrews and Jordan 1993; Hairston and Smith 1983), thus adding further rationale for integration to improve the self- and racial esteem of African American deaf children.

The Training of African American Teachers for the Deaf

According to Doctor (1948), a large number of teachers of the African American deaf were White despite the fact that administrators sought out better-qualified Black teachers to educate the deaf members of their own race. Their number, however, was very limited (Jowers 2005). In fact, White teachers were employed in several states, including at the Alabama School for the Negro Deaf, the Maryland School for the Colored Deaf and Blind, the Negro Department in the Kentucky School for the Deaf, and the Tennessee School for the Deaf Colored Department (Higgins and Doctor 1951).

Statistics regarding the work of Black teachers with Black deaf and hard of hearing students are difficult to find. Settles (1940) reported on a questionnaire that was sent to 16 institutions for the deaf that had schools or departments specifically for the Black deaf. While all 16 schools replied, one school failed to give the rates of attendance. Responses from 15 schools indicated that there were 837 Black pupils (428 males and 409 females) who were taught by 81 teachers (22 males and 59 females). In addition, the questionnaire revealed that of the 81 teachers, 48 were college graduates, 18 had two years of college, and 15 were high school graduates. Many schools recruited teachers from HBCUs. However, despite shared ethnicity, many of these teachers had little education or experience in methods of teaching deaf students (Flowers 1915). Mary Herring Wright, a graduate of the North Carolina school, comments directly on this issue. She describes one teacher as "never bothering to really learn the signs. She mostly made up her own signs and her motions were quick and jerky. We had to teach all of the new teachers how to sign" (1999, 211). Ties between HBCUs and Black deaf schools were broken when desegregation resulted in the closure of the Black schools and the pupils were sent into formerly all White schools (Lane, Hoffmeister, and Bahan 1996). Table 2.3 shows the relationships between a number of HBCUs and Black deaf schools.

According to Brill (1950), the problem was not addressed until Superintendent E. A. Gruver of the Pennsylvania School discussed it in his address as president of the Convention of American Instructors of the Deaf (CAID) at its twenty-seventh meeting in 1931. He said, "The Convention should inaugurate a movement to assist the Negro teacher in receiving the benefits of the established training classes, summer schools and other activities" (cited in Brill 1950, 91). Superintendent Gruver employed Black teachers but found it difficult to recruit Black teachers trained to work with the deaf. He urged that a program be established to provide the training teachers would need to succeed: "It seems to me that provision should be made for the systematic training of Negro young men and women in the theory and practice of the oral method of instruction as well as the general theory of teaching the deaf, so that they can train their own people later" (1931, 367–68).

A special training center for Black teachers of the deaf was started at West Virginia State College in Institute in 1938. In 1942 the training

Table 2.3. Teacher Recruitment by Schools for the African American Deaf at Historically Black Colleges/Universities

Schools for the "Colored/Negro" Deaf	Historically Black Colleges/Universities
Kendall School for the Deaf	Howard University
North Carolina State School for the Deaf and Blind	Shaw University
Alabama School for the Negro Deaf and Blind	Talladega College
Virginia School for the Colored Deaf	Hampton University
West Virginia School for the Colored Deaf	West Virginia State College
Florida State School for the Deaf	Florida A&M University
Southern State School for the Deaf	Southern State University
Mississippi School for the Negro Deaf	Jackson State University
Arkansas School for the Colored Deaf and Blind (Madison School)	Philander Smith College

center for Black teachers of both the blind and the deaf was transferred to Hampton Institute in Virginia (Doctor 1948; Fusfeld 1941). Another training class for Black teachers of the deaf was conducted at Southern University near Baton Rouge, Louisiana (Netterville 1938). During the summer of 1948, 267 students were enrolled at Hampton in the curriculum for the special education of the deaf and the hard of hearing. Staff members from Gallaudet College taught during the summers of 1948 and 1949 (Vale 1948). Courses were arranged over a period of several years so the students at Hampton University could earn both a bachelor's and a master's degree in special education (Brill 1950).

Even in the late twentieth century, the teaching staff in schools and programs for deaf children was still about 90 percent White (Andrews and

Jordan 1993; Cohen, Fischgrund, and Redding 1990; Mobley 1991). In a 1993 survey of 6,043 professionals in 349 deaf education programs, Andrews and Jordan (1993) found that the number of minority teachers and professionals in deaf education was very low, constituting only about 10.4 percent of the total, and that, of those minority professionals, only 11.7 percent were deaf. Redding (1997) raises the question of whether the low numbers reflect a continued resistance to change or the lack of a large pool of qualified minority candidates.

The Role of Oralism

Oralism, the belief that spoken language is inherently superior to sign language, played an important role in deaf education. Even though deaf education in the United States began in 1817 with sign language as the medium of instruction, by 1880 the oral method of instruction was well established in the White schools (Lane, Hoffmeister, and Bahan 1996). As Burch and Joyner note, "the rise of oralism motivated schools across the country to replace deaf teachers with hearing instructors who would speak to students rather than sign with them" (2007, 21). However, oral education was not extended to Black deaf students on the same basis as it was to White deaf students. According to Settles (1940), eleven of sixteen schools or departments for Black deaf students surveyed still used an entirely manual approach (i.e., signing) (Baynton 1996). In 1920, three-fourths of the children at the Texas White school were being taught orally, while less than one-third of the children at the Black school were being taught orally (Baynton 1996, 46). Baynton notes: "Because of the continued use of sign language in the classroom, however, the ironic result of this policy of discrimination may have been that southern deaf African Americans, in spite of the chronic underfunding of their schools, received a better education than most deaf White students" (1996, 180). Nevertheless, although some African American children received more comprehensible instruction than White children, they were still placed in vocational rather than academic tracks. Moreover, the facilities for White children were far superior to those for Black children. Wright, for example, describes a visit to the school for White blind children:

"[W]e were given a tour of their campus and the differences between their school and ours were unbelievable. . . . [S]eeing such a difference in how the White children were treated and how we were treated at the Black state school left us depressed and angry" (1999, 179–80).

Oralism did have an impact on the education of some our study participants who were forbidden to use ASL and forced to use speech in the classroom even though their speech was unintelligible. One school in this study, the North Carolina School for the Colored Deaf and Blind, supported the oral method, and both teachers and students were forbidden to use ASL in the classroom. Participants in the study said that it drastically hampered their learning and affected their academic achievement. However, outside of the classroom, the students continued to use ASL.

What Language Did Children from Black Deaf Families Bring to School?

The third factor concerns the language the children brought with them to the school. There were a considerable number of Black deaf families who used signing that their children brought with them to school. These children no doubt served as sign models, as did White children from deaf families (Lane, Hoffmeister, and Bahan 1996). There were also many children from hearing nonsigning families. We examined this question with emphasis on the children from Black deaf families. Several participants from Louisiana, Alabama, Virginia, and Texas are from multigenerational deaf families. In the interviews, they discussed learning signs from their parents and their grandparents. This is a ripe area for systematic research as there has been very little work on Black deaf parents and their deaf children.

BLACK DEAF SCHOOLS AT THE SIX RESEARCH SITES

We mentioned earlier that seventeen states and the District of Columbia had segregated schools for deaf children.[7] In this section we outline the history of the six schools in the states where we collected data: (1) the North Carolina State School for the Colored Deaf and Blind, established in 1868–1869 in Raleigh; (2) the Arkansas Department for the Colored Deaf and Blind, established in Little Rock in 1887; (3) the Asylum for Colored Youths and Orphans, established in Austin in 1887; (4) the Alabama School for the Negro Deaf and Blind, established in 1892 in Talladega; (5) the Virginia State School for the Colored Deaf and Blind, established in 1909 in Newport News; and (6) the Louisiana State School for the Negro Deaf and Blind, established in Baton Rouge in 1938. The schools, ranging from the first school established for Black deaf students to the most recent, represent a cross-section of the types of education available to these students. They also represent the different regions of the South, ranging from the Deep South sites of Alabama and Louisiana to the inland south of Arkansas and the coastal areas of Virginia.

The North Carolina State School for the Colored Deaf and Blind

The North Carolina State School for the Deaf and Blind, established in 1845, was the ninth school in the United States to provide education for blind and deaf students. However, because this was during the era of slavery, the administrators provided education only for White students (Crockett and Crockett-Dease 1990).

The older North Carolina participants were former students of the North Carolina School for the Colored Deaf and Blind. Like all southern Black children, Black deaf children were unschooled until after the Civil War. In 1867, two years after the end of the war, the North Carolina assembly acknowledged a lack of education for Black deaf and blind individuals. In 1868 the legislature enacted a provision for the education of Black deaf children, thereby becoming the first state to provide an institution for this population, following Gallaudet's Kendall School for the

---

7. Many of the schools for Black Deaf children experienced name changes. The Texas school, for example, had five names between 1887 and 1965. We have tried to use the correct name for the period being discussed.

Deaf (KSD) in the District of Columbia. The School for the Colored Deaf, Dumb, and Blind officially opened its doors on January 7, 1869, in Raleigh with twenty-one deaf and seven blind Black students (Crockett and Crockett-Dease 1990; Gannon 1981). William Holden, governor and Unionist during Reconstruction, supported the founding of the North Carolina school for White deaf children during a previous term. Given his vigorous attempts to guarantee citizenship rights for former slaves and his vigorous campaign against the Ku Klux Klan, which eventually led to his impeachment (*Houston Daily Union* 1871), it is perhaps not surprising that he also supported the founding of a school for Black deaf children.

In contrast to the KSD, in North Carolina, vocational training was emphasized at the expense of developing academic skills and scholarship. The situation was unique in that there were three different campuses to serve the White blind and deaf population, whereas the Raleigh campus (housing the Blacks) served the entire state. Desegregation did not begin in earnest until the 1960s. Combining the blind and the deaf schools served as a catalyst for the teachers to improve themselves professionally in the two respective areas of their professional expertise, "blindness and deafness" (Crockett and Crockett-Dease 1990).

The name of the Black institution was changed to the North Carolina State School for the Blind and Deaf (NCSSBD) in 1905.

In 1945 the name was changed again, this time to the Governor Morehead School, in honor of John Motley Morehead, who had played a pivotal role in establishing the school (Crockett and Crockett-Dease 1990). Because of its address, the school is most commonly referred to as the Garner Road School.

In 1954, when the Supreme Court ruled that public school segregation was unconstitutional, North Carolina faculty and staff reacted in various ways. They did not fear federal law because enforcement was lax and change was not enforced until the 1960s. School administrators, however, faced dwindling funds to support their programs. They finally cooperated, however, and integration took place. The newly integrated schools became eligible for funds from the federal government for academic and

Figure 2.2. The North Carolina State School for the Blind and Deaf. (Photograph courtesy of Gallaudet University Archives. Used by permission.)

extracurricular activities programs that similarly situated schools had been receiving for years (Crockett and Crockett-Dease 1990).

The majority of Black deaf students followed vocational courses offered to the average high school student. The male students were trained to work skillfully in the areas of woodworking, industrial arts, printing, and shoe repair. Female students were taught typing, sewing, cosmetology, and culinary science (Crockett and Crockett-Dease 1990).

According to Crockett and Crockett-Dease (1990), Black deaf children in the NCSSBD were handicapped "by their color" because they were not permitted to go beyond the tenth grade or to attend the school for White deaf children at the NCSSBD located in Morganton, North Carolina, to complete their high school education. This also disqualified them from attending Gallaudet College. However, some changes were eventually made: "Therefore as we progressed in the teaching of our students, another grade was added to our curriculum and several students [were] permitted to continue with their training in efforts to become qualified to attend Gallaudet College" (Crockett and Crockett-Dease 1990, 11). The school was fully integrated in June 1967 (Crockett and Crockett-Dease 1990).

The Arkansas Department for the Colored Deaf and Blind

The first school for White deaf children in Arkansas opened in 1850 in Clarksville. In 1867, the city of Little Rock also established a school for White deaf children, and the following year (on July 17, 1868), the state legislature incorporated the school as a state institution and named it the Arkansas Deaf-Mute Institute (Bevill and Vollmar 1975). The name was later changed to the Arkansas School for the Deaf and Blind (ASD).

The year 1887 marked several milestones for ASD. First, the teachers and matrons had dual roles. They not only taught in the classroom but also cared for the children with the help of monitors, who were appointed from among the older and more trustworthy students. Second, when the enrollment passed the one hundred mark, the administration instituted the policy of having full-time supervisors for the students. The matrons and the supervisor provided the "home life" for the children and took care of them when they were not in class. A third milestone was the addition of a separate building and department for Black deaf students on the campus. A Black matron and teacher named Pleasant A. Glenn was hired to care for the Black students. Ned F. Bennett was the first Black pupil at the school, which many of the Arkansas participants in this study attended. Later, in 1925, the legislature enacted a compulsory attendance law (Riggs 1934, 31), which required that every deaf or blind child who could not benefit from attending a public school be sent to ASD. The law also mandated that Black children be placed in a separate school located at a place designated by the State Board of Control (Riggs 1934).

In 1926 a new school for Black deaf students was built because of the dilapidated condition of the school built in 1887. Figure 2.3 shows the original Black school.

During the 1930s and 1940s, two White deaf educators served as principals of the "Colored Department." Also during this period, most of the teachers who taught in the "Colored Department" were White (Anderson 2006). In the late 1940s, there was strong opposition in Arkansas to school integration both in the public schools and the schools for the deaf and blind. This resulted in a 1949 decision to build a new $200,000 school for Black deaf students at 22nd and Madison streets, some distance away from the ASD campus. The new facility on Madison Street provided classroom, dormitory, and dining space for Black deaf and blind boys and girls. It also included apartment space for the school principal (Anderson 2006; Bevill and Vollmar 1975).

Figure 2.3. The "Colored" Department of the Arkansas School for the Deaf, at left. (Photograph courtesy of Gallaudet University Archives. Used by permission.)

In the fall of 1950, the Black deaf and blind students were moved to the new school building on Madison Street, which became known as the Madison School (see figure 2.4). A Black principal, Edward Gordon, who moved from the "Colored Department" on the ASD campus, was hired to supervise the school, which had an enrollment of thirty-six deaf and twenty-five blind students (Anderson 2006; Bevill and Vollmar 1975). However, the board of trustees and the superintendent retained full authority over the school.

The second principal was a hearing Black man named I. C. Phillips. He had graduated from Philander Smith College, an HBCU in Little Rock, and then taught for six years at the Missouri School for the Deaf in Fulton before becoming the principal at Madison. Phillips recruited education majors from Philander Smith to teach at Madison School.

Black deaf students were integrated into the ASD campus in 1965, thus ending the history of the Madison School. Some of the teachers also

Figure 2.4. Teachers and students of the Madison Street School in 1950. (Photograph courtesy of Glenn Anderson. Used by permission.)

transferred to work at the Arkansas School for the Deaf. "It was so impor-tant to have some of the teachers from the Deaf Department go with our kids." Unfortunately, some of the other staff members' careers ended when the schools integrated (Anderson 2006, 17).

Texas Asylum for Deaf, Dumb, and Blind Colored Youth

In 1856 the Texas Institution for the Education of the Deaf and Dumb was created for White deaf students. The name was changed to the Texas Deaf and Dumb Institution around 1868, to the Texas Institution for the Deaf and Dumb about 1871, and to the Texas Deaf and Dumb Asylum about 1887. Finally, in 1911, the name was changed to its current designa-tion, the Texas School for the Deaf (TSD) (Smyrl 2001).

The Texas legislature created the Asylum for Deaf and Dumb and Blind Colored Youth in 1887 in Austin. "The Legislature felt the necessity of establishing a school because of their being Deaf, the colored youth could not reap the benefits of the public schools and because of their race could not attend the White schools" (Fay 1893). Three more name changes followed: in 1943, to the State School for Deaf and Blind Negro Children; in 1947, to the Texas Blind, Deaf, and Orphan School (BDO); and in 1965, to the Texas Blind and Deaf School (Smyrl 2001). Some of the proj-ect participants attended the BDO school. The original 1887 school is shown in figure 2.5.

Governor Lawrence S. Ross appointed William H. Holland, shown in figure 2.6, as the school's first superintendent on August 15, 1887 (Brewer 1935/1970; Logan and Winston 1982). Holland, a man with many tal-ents, was born a slave in 1841 in Marshall, Texas (Tabak 2006). A soldier, legislator, humanitarian, visionary, and an educator, he was instrumental in getting the Texas legislature to pass a bill to establish the Asylum for Deaf, Dumb, and Blind Colored Youth. Holland also established Prairie View Normal College, now Prairie View A&M University, an institution that admitted Deaf students seeking degrees in higher education programs (tsl.state.tx.us; Tabak 2006).

Figure 2.5. The Asylum for Colored Deaf and Dumb and Blind Colored Youth. (Photograph courtesy of Gallaudet University Archives. Used by permission.)

Figure 2.6. William H. Holland, the founder of the Texas Asylum for Colored Youths and Orphans. (Photograph courtesy of Betty Henderson. Used by permission.)

Holland served as superintendent for two periods, 1887–1897 and 1904–1907. The school opened in April 1888 with an enrollment of 31, of whom 23 were deaf and 8 were blind. By 1890, the enrollment had grown to 68 students; 38 were deaf, and 30 were blind.

The school was exceptional in that its staff included several Black deaf teachers. Also, the school opened its first session with one Black deaf teacher, Julius Garrett, who stayed for one year. A second Black deaf teacher, Amanda A. Johnson, was hired later. Both Garrett and Johnson were graduates of the North Carolina School for the Colored Deaf and Blind (Gannon 1981; Tabak 2006). A third hard of hearing Black man named H. L. Johns was hired. Johns, a graduate of the Maryland School for Colored Deaf, taught older students. Finally, in 1900 Holland also hired a hearing Black teacher, Mattie B. Haywood.

Somewhat later a fourth Black deaf teacher, Otis Massey was hired under a different administration. Massey was one of three Black deaf men accepted at Gallaudet College in the early 1950s. He was very popular with the students and an excellent role model. He was the only Deaf faculty member during the period he taught in Texas and the only one who could sign fluently (Tabak 2006).

We have no firm information on how or why Holland became involved with deaf and blind children. Nevertheless, it is clear that he possessed a great deal of compassion, with very positive attitudes about deafness, blindness, and race. He believed in the students' ability to learn. In several of his 1894 reports, he indicated that he was the superintendent of a school, an educational institution, *not* an asylum (Tabak 2006).

Despite Holland's willingness to employ Deaf teachers, in the first year, most of the teachers were hearing with the exception of one deaf male. The hearing teachers, all of whom were Black, were not fluent in sign language. The students learned signed language from their Black deaf teachers, who were originally from North Carolina. However, the students were taught via the combined method of instruction, a system that used both sign language and the oral method. Students were also provided speech classes in addition to reading, writing, language, history, composition, arithmetic, geography, and physiology (Tabak 2006).

Holland had high expectations and encouraged the students to excel academically. His goals were to provide the students with the benefits of a liberal education. In his first year, the students were taught Latin, algebra, and geometry. However, the trustees frowned on this curriculum, and Holland faced immense pressure to provide students with no more than the most basic academic classes. Later the focus was shifted to "industrial training," which consisted of sewing, crocheting and fancy needlework, shoemaking, and mechanics. There was no preparation for college (Tabak 2006).

In 1943, the State Colored Orphans Home closed, and the administration moved the children to the institute, which was merged with the Texas Blind, Deaf, and Orphan School (BDO). Most of the Black deaf children were not orphans, although the Black hearing children were. According to Tabak (2006), all of the employees were Black except the medical staff.

After the merger, the blind, deaf, and orphan students attended separate classes. Nevertheless, the experience of being part of the same school community created a unique cultural experience for the Black deaf and hearing students. The latter were exposed to Deaf culture and learned signed language. The Deaf students became used to signing with hearing children. Their experience was in stark contrast to their White deaf counterparts. When interviewed, Black hearing and Deaf alumni commented fondly that these formative years had "widened their views of the world" (Tabak 2006,108).

The BDO was finally integrated with the Texas School for the Deaf (TSD) in 1966. The transition proved difficult for the faculty and students because of the inferior education they had received at the BDO. They were not prepared for the academic curriculum at the TSD.

The Alabama School for the Negro Deaf and Blind

In October 1858 Dr. Joseph H. Johnson, a White hearing man, founded the Alabama Institution for the Deaf and Dumb; "Blind" was added to the name in 1869. However, no provision was made for the education of Black deaf children in that state until 1891, when the state legislature authorized Dr. Johnson to start a program. According to Crouch and Hawkins (1983), the first officially expressed concern for the education of Black deaf Alabamians was recorded in the minutes of the institute's board on New Year's Day of 1881, when "the matter of providing for the education of colored deaf, mute, and the blind children was brought to the attention of the Board" (52). It was unanimously agreed at the meeting that the state should provide for their education.

The Alabama School for the Negro Deaf and Blind (later, ASNDB) opened January 4, 1892, with 9 students. By November of that first year, 54 were enrolled, 33 of whom were deaf and 21 of whom were blind (Alabama Institute for the Deaf and Blind 1892). Initially, the Black deaf and the Black blind were housed together on the same campus (Bardes 1952; Crouch and Hawkins 1983). Figure 2.7 shows the school as it appeared in the nineteenth century.

Figure 2.7. The Alabama School for Negro Deaf and Blind in the early years. (Photograph courtesy of Gallaudet University Archives. Used by permission.)

The school's industrial department was considered the most important because "all of our pupils after leaving school must depend upon manual labor for their support" (Bardes 1952, 40). In 1894, instruction in the following trades was offered: carpentry, upholstery, chair caning, and gardening for boys, and sewing, cooking, and housework for girls. Shoe repair and piano tuning were in the planning stages, and a laundry (completed in 1895) offered still another training area (Alabama Institute for the Deaf and Blind 1894). Eventually, the ASNDB had the largest enrollment of Black deaf students of any school in the nation. In 1950–1951, 202 pupils were enrolled, although, the *American Annals of the Deaf (AAD)* recorded only 175 as of October 31, 1950 (Bardes 1952). The administrators at the Alabama School for Black students believed that their educational task was to provide training in the use of English, to help the students develop an identity of self as well as of social environment, to teach communicative skills acceptable to the hearing world, and to overcome racial prejudice by developing the students' competence in socially accepted goals. Their charge was also to address health and safety, vocational training, family, citizenship, and leisure time (Bardes 1952). The Alabama Vocational Rehabilitation Service stated that Black deaf girls, who were taught laundering, cooking, and sewing, were their hardest placement problems. The boys were taught mechanical arts, dairy arts, and barbering. There was no mention of preparing students for college. Rather, it was the school's policy to prepare the students for employment instead of higher education. The school, therefore, was vocational only. The administrator justified the decision to focus on vocation training as follows:

> The fundamental aspect of the school is not neglected. . . . [I]t is a school for Negroes. The pupils are not to be ashamed of their race. They have a fine heritage to emulate. They are deaf [and] their conduct should be such that deaf people generally should be respected not pitied nor ridiculed. (Bardes 1952, 6)

The ultimate goal of the AIDB administrators was to teach their charges to understand their citizenship and the ways in which they would live, communicate, have families, work, play, and cooperate intelligently. The philosophy of the school was expressed in the actions of the pupils, who strove for full acceptance into society on their own merits and enjoyed the process (Bardes 1952).

Changes were slow to occur following the *Brown v. Board of Education* decision, especially in Alabama. Administrators at the AIDB faced the question of educating Blacks and Whites together with great reluctance. They had experienced complaints regarding segregation throughout the 1960s. Concern about jeopardizing federal funding was reflected in the board's minutes (Crouch and Hawkins 1983).

The parents of a Black deaf student filed a lawsuit against the school's segregation policy, and in September 1967 the U.S. District Court heard the case of *Christine Archie vs. Alabama Institute for the Deaf and Blind*. In the resulting decision, the court ordered the institute to file a plan for desegregation by December 20, 1967. The court order called for the end of segregation of classes, faculty, and programs. Upset White parents and administrators met with officials in Governor George Wallace's office, and the governor's legal advisor assured them that the attorney general's office would defend the institute's position (Crouch and Hawkins 1983).

The school attorneys for the AIDB tried to defend the school. They presented an alternative desegregation plan to U.S. District Court Judge H. H. Grooms in late December of 1967. The judge approved the plan, but the plaintiff rejected it. The court of appeal reversed Grooms's decision and ordered the institute to integrate every facet of its operation. In July 1968 Superintendent E. H. Gentry submitted his final plan for desegregation of the Alabama Institute for the Deaf and Blind (Crouch and Hawkins 1983; Plans for Desegregation, AIDB Archives 1967, 1968; minutes, AIDB Archives, Sept. 1, 1967).

According to the plan, the institute had to be fully integrated by September of 1968. Superintendent E. H. Gentry had presented several desegregation plans before retiring. He called for transferring fifteen Black blind students and about ten Black deaf students to the formerly all-White schools for the blind and deaf, respectively. The revised plan also included transferring at least one Black teacher of the deaf to the White school for the deaf. The integration of the elementary schools was to be carried out in subsequent years (Crouch and Hawkins 1983).

The eleventh president of the Alabama Institute for the Deaf and Blind, Dr. W. W. Elliott, had the enormous responsibility of carrying out the court's orders to fully integrate the schools by September 1968. Dr. Elliott encountered major problems in implementing the integration plan in the fall of 1968, including dissensions between Black and White parents. Some parents of lower-functioning White children resented their children's placement on the former Negro campus and again asked Governor George Wallace to intervene (Elliott correspondence, October 7, 1968, in Crouch and Hawkins 1983, 240). On the other hand, parents of a Black child filed suit challenging the institute's continued segregation of the elementary grades. The Black parents won their suit, and the institute was eventually forced to pay $4,300 in legal fees incurred by the complaining parents (minutes, AIDB Archives, May 15, 1969).

The Virginia State School for the Colored Deaf and Blind

The Virginia legislature established the Virginia School for the Deaf and Blind (VSDB) for White children in Staunton. The school opened on November 15, 1839. There was no provision for the education of Black deaf children until one man took it upon himself to fight for their cause in 1902.

William Charles Ritter, shown in figure 2.8, an alumnus of the Virginia School for the Deaf and Gallaudet College, was the only White deaf person to establish a school for Black deaf children. Deeply moved by the plight of many uneducated Black deaf people whom he met, he decided to do something about it. He approached a friend who was a legislator and asked for assistance in drafting a bill for a school. Harry Rutherford Houston assisted Ritter in drafting the appropriation to establish a school for the Negro deaf and blind in Newport News. The bill was presented to the

Figure 2.8. William Charles Ritter, the founder of the Virginia State School for the Colored Deaf and Blind. (Photograph courtesy of Gallaudet University Archives. Used by permission.)

legislature in 1902 but not enacted. It was revised several times in the House and Senate before it was finally approved in 1908. In 1909, the board of visitors elected Ritter as the first superintendent of the school (*Silent Worker* 1909).

The first session in Newport News began on September 8, 1909, with twenty students. Ritter taught the first class. His wife, Leslie Ritter, a graduate of the North Carolina School, also assisted him with teaching at the school. The student population, which included both deaf and blind children, eventually increased to two hundred. Figure 2.9 shows the school in the early years of the twentieth century.

William Ritter remained at the school until 1937. In 1947 the school was renamed the Virginia State School at Newport News. Ritter's distinguished career included an honorary degree from Gallaudet College,

VIRGINIA STATE SCHOOL FOR COLORED DEAF AND BLIND, NEWPORT NEWS, VA.

Figure 2.9. The Virginia State School for Colored Deaf and Blind in the early twentieth century.

which recognized his work on behalf of Black deaf and blind children with an honorary master of arts on June 10, 1930 (Bass 1949).

Integration of the White school at Staunton and the Black school, which had moved from Newport News to nearby Hampton, began in the 1960s. According to Yates:

> Both the Hampton and Staunton schools were partially integrated by 1965. The first African American pupil to enroll at the Staunton School was Larry Laverne Fortune of Charlottesville, whose parents transferred him from the Hampton School in August, 1965. At the time Larry was eleven years old. The second Black student was thirteen-year-old William Whiteside of Roanoke, who enrolled in 1966. William had lost his hearing while in the Roanoke public school system. He had more difficulty in adjusting and remarked that he felt that some of the students resented him because he was Black.

Both William and Larry completed the school program.
(2004, 2)

In 1967, the U.S. Department of Health, Education, and Welfare and the Office for Civil Rights of the U.S. Department of Justice investigated the Staunton and Hampton schools. Yates records that "A *Washington Post* newspaper article called their attention to the fact that both schools had a racially identifiable school population. While conducting an investigation, the Federal offices came down hard on the two schools and on the two Boards of Visitors" (2004, 2). The schools' administrators set up a task force to address a plan for integration. In reply to the task force's plan for integration, Peter E. Holmes, director of the Office for Civil Rights, wrote to Governor Holton in August 1973 and stated the following:

> We have carefully reviewed the plans which Mr. Otis Brown, Secretary of Human Affairs, submitted on July 13 to bring the Virginia Schools for the Deaf and Blind at Hampton and Staunton into compliance with Title VI of the Civil Rights Act of 1964. With respect to the student assignment, the plan basically calls for Interstate 95 serving as the one line between the schools, with all students to the east assigned to Hampton and to the West (including Richmond), to Staunton. As a result, the 1973–74 enrollment at Hampton was expected to be 65 percent black, while the non-White enrollment at Staunton was approximately 25 percent. (cited in Yates 2004, 2)

By 1975, out of a total of 184 staff members, Hampton had 27 White employees. The student body was 67 percent Black. At Staunton there were only 10 Black workers on a staff of 242. During that same period, the racial composition of grades K–8 at Staunton reached 62 Black pupils and 156 White students (Yates 2004, 3).

In 2006, the General Assembly decided to consolidate the Hampton school and the Virginia School for the Deaf and Blind in Staunton on the Staunton campus (*Hearing Loss* 2008). In June 2008, after ninety-nine years in existence, the Virginia School for the Deaf, Blind, and Multi-disabled in Hampton was closed.

The Southern School for Deaf Negroes

The Louisiana State School for the Deaf (LSSD) for White students opened on December 8, 1852, with eleven pupils in attendance. Originally known as the "Louisiana Institution for the Deaf and Dumb and the Blind" and often referred to as an "asylum," the school's history reflects the evolution of Deaf education in the United States. In 1908, the name was changed to the "Louisiana State School for the Deaf" (LSSD) (Netterville 1938).

Some of the project participants from New Orleans had attended the State School for Deaf Negroes. Provision for the education of the Black deaf students did not occur until eighty-six years after the White school was established, when the State of Louisiana passed a bill to create the State School for Deaf Negroes (known as SSD) in 1938 in Scotlandville. The state appropriated $10,000 a year for its support and maintenance, but as there was no building, this amount passed into a building fund supplemented by Southern University and A&M College. It was through the efforts of Dr. J. S. Clark that funds were provided to support the school. At the time, Dr. Clark was president of Southern University. The SSD was located on the university campus in Baton Rouge, and the university president served as its superintendent.

According to Netterville (1938), prior to his retirement in 1938, Dr. Clark selected a faculty member, E. L. Gordon Sr. to serve as principal. Gordon was the son of F. M. Gordon, who had been the principal of the Georgia School for the Colored Deaf Department for forty-six years. He was also an experienced administrator who had been the head teacher in the Negro Department of the Mississippi School (1937–1940) and the Negro Department of the Georgia School for the Deaf.

In 1938, the school was in a one-story brick building with an operational budget of $10,000 and a faculty of nine (figure 2.10). The student enrollment was forty-four. As the program developed, additional space was added for a dining hall, kitchen, two guest rooms, two social rooms, and

Figure 2.10. The staff of the State School for the Deaf Negroes (Louisiana) in 1938. (Photograph courtesy of the Archives Department, John B. Cade Library, Southern University and A&M College, Baton Rouge, La. Used by permission.)

an assembly room. By 1951–1952 the annual operational budget reached $102,740.00, and enrollment had increased to ninety-four students (Netterville 1938).

The school used the combined method of instruction. Fingerspelling, script print, speech, and lipreading were provided, and speech was taught in classrooms that had auditory equipment. The school adopted the public school courses of study, as well as special courses for the deaf. Students were provided three years of prevocational training to prepare them to select a particular trade. Vocational programs included shoe repairing, woodwork, cosmetology, and home economics. Students were given instruction in at least two of the trades taught (Bradford 1943). Figure 2.11, a photo of an early sewing class, illustrates the type of education offered.

In 1978, the LSSD merged with the State School for Deaf Negroes (SSD), and the joined entities became known as the Louisiana School for the Deaf (LSD). Today, the Louisiana Board of Elementary and Secondary Education (BESE) manages the school.

Figure 2.11. Sewing class for girls at the Southern School for Deaf Negroes. (Photograph courtesy of the Archives Department, John B. Cade Library, Southern University and A&M College, Baton Rouge, La. Used by permission.)

SUMMARY

Many factors influenced the development of Black ASL. In particular, teachers, whether deaf or hearing, Black or White, played a significant role in deaf children's education. Comments from the project participants show how diverse the teachers were. For example, participants from the North Carolina School for the Colored Deaf recalled one Black deaf teacher who signed to them in the classroom. Participants from the BDO in Austin were fortunate to have several Black deaf teachers at different times during the school's history. Participants from the Madison Street school in Little Rock had Black and White hearing teachers, while participants from the Alabama School for the Negro Deaf had Black and White deaf and hearing teachers. The teachers used sign language in the classrooms. Participants from the Virginia School for the Colored Deaf highly praised William Ritter, a White deaf man. They also had Black and White deaf and hearing teachers. Finally, the participants from the Southern School for the Deaf in Louisiana commented on their frustration at not being allowed to use sign language in the classroom.

From the beginning of Black deaf education in the South, then, the nature of the input the children received varied both from state to state and within states. These varied sources of input included White ASL, homesign systems, the signing brought to residential schools by Black deaf children from deaf families, spoken southern White English, and southern African American English. All of these sources influenced the language variety that this book explores.

In this chapter, we have seen how social history and geographical isolation impacted the lives of Black deaf students. Although many Black deaf children were exposed to signed language in the classroom, they nevertheless attended segregated schools and received an unequal education; in particular, the facilities at their schools were not on a par with those that White children enjoyed. Their exposure to oralism was mixed. The combination of factors in the segregated schools created the conditions for the development of a unique sign language variety that was distinct from that used by White deaf students.

Research Methods

The study of language variation requires the collection and analysis of data—real language produced by signers or speakers in a variety of contexts—from a representative sample of the community whose language we are studying. Therefore, in conducting the research, we created data-collection conditions conducive to the production of Black ASL. The main components of the data collection are the sites, the signers, the contact persons, and the settings for filming: group sessions, interviews, and elicited narratives. In this chapter, we describe how we collected the data for this project: how we selected communities and recruited signers, the role of community-based contact people in data collection, and how the filming was done. We also describe the analyses that we conducted, the results of which are reported in chapters 4 through 8, and the two corpora that we created based on the data tapes used for the analyses of the size of the signing space, constructed action and constructed dialogue, mouthing, and repetition.

SITES, PARTICIPANTS, AND DATA COLLECTION

The Sites

Based on the findings reported in Lucas, Bayley, and Valli (2001), we hypothesized that the kind of school the signers attended would have a direct bearing on their language use. Signers for the project were therefore recruited according to whether they had attended segregated or desegregated programs. This means that we filmed signers who were 55 or older and by definition went to segregated schools and signers who were 35 or younger and attended integrated schools. In our analyses we took into account the fact that a few of the participants first attended segregated schools and later moved to integrated ones.

As chapter 2 points out, seventeen states and the District of Columbia had segregated schools or departments for Black deaf children. The available resources did not allow us to film in all eighteen locations, so we chose six, ranging from North Carolina, the state with the first school for Black deaf children, to Louisiana, which did not establish a school until the second third of the twentieth century.

Figure 3.1 is a map of the six states in which data were collected. In North Carolina, Arkansas, Alabama, and Virginia, we were able to film at or near the former school for Black deaf children. Participants in Texas and Louisiana were filmed at sites not affiliated with the schools, and one group of Louisiana participants consisted of people who had moved to Houston in 2005 following Hurricane Katrina, which devastated much of southern Louisiana.

Another factor that shaped the data collection was the sensitivity of the signers to the audiological status and ethnicity of the audience. The

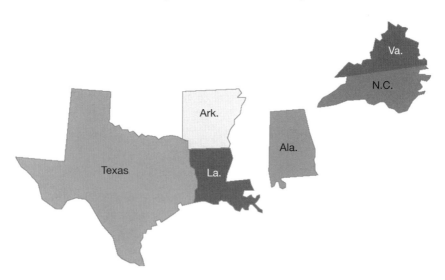

Figure 3.1. Map of states where data were collected.

amount of attention that language users pay to their language production has been addressed by sociolinguists, starting with Labov (1972b), who discussed to what he referred to as the "observer's paradox." That is, our interest is the language that signers and speakers use when they are not being observed. However, to obtain the kind of data that we need for analysis we need to record the signers' (or speakers') production in situations that often lead to self-consciousness. The problem is particularly acute in sign linguistics because, on video, there is no way that signers can be completely anonymous. In addition, as scholars who have discussed the influence of audience design on language use have shown (see, e.g., Bell 1984, 2001; Giles 1973, 2001; Giles and Powesland 1975), speakers and signers often adjust their language use to accommodate to what they perceive as the preference of their interlocutors. To overcome the problem of the observer's paradox and to encourage language users to employ the vernacular, or their everyday, unmonitored language, Labov (1972b, 1984) developed the sociolinguistic interview. In contrast to most interview schedules, the sociolinguistic interview consists of a number of modules dealing with topics designed to put the researcher in a "one-down" (i.e., less powerful) position in relation to the interviewee. Since the goal is to obtain as much informal language production as possible, the researcher is not concerned with the truth value of the responses, nor is there any need for interviewees to respond to all of the questions—or for the researcher to work through all of them. Questions are brief and avoid learned or school language in favor of informal, everyday speech. Typical questions concern childhood games, dating patterns, marriage and family, dreams, and the famous "danger of death" question (i.e., "Have you ever been in a situation where you were in serious danger of getting killed, where you said to yourself, 'This is it!'?"). In spoken language studies, researchers have also found that having interviewers who share the same ethnicity as the interviewee may also result in more informal language (Rickford and McNair-Knox 1994).

In sign linguistics, Lucas and Valli (1992) demonstrated that ASL users are very sensitive to an interviewer's audiological status and ethnicity (i.e., hearing or deaf, Black or White). This sensitivity may be manifested by rapid switching from ASL to Signed English (a manual code for English) or contact signing (an outcome of the contact between ASL and English, characterized by core features from both languages and continuous voiceless mouthing). As explained by Giles's accommodation theory, (1973) many Deaf people will adjust their signing to bring it closer to what they perceive to be the preference of their interlocutor. In Lucas, Bayley, and Valli (2001), Black signers were recorded with no White researchers present and interviewed by a Black deaf interviewer in an attempt to minimize the observer's paradox. Nevertheless, while the lexical elicitation task showed clear differences between Black and White choices, the Black signers in the study appeared to have shifted to a more standard ASL. In addition, with the exception of signers from Louisiana, the Black signers in Lucas, Bayley, and Valli (2001) were from Boston, Kansas City, and California. For the project we report on here, all of the interviews were also conducted by Black researchers, all of the participants were residents of the South, and many had attended segregated schools, so we may well see different results.

As explained earlier, data were collected in six sites, selected according to when the schools for Black deaf children were founded: Raleigh, North Carolina; Little Rock, Arkansas; Houston, Texas; Talladega, Alabama; Hampton, Virginia; and New Orleans, Louisiana. Raleigh, Talladega, Little Rock, and Hampton are the sites of former schools for Black deaf children, and all but Hampton were the sites of integrated schools for deaf children at the time of data collection.[8] Houston and New Orleans have large and stable Black deaf communities. In addition, attendees at the 2007 National Black Deaf Advocates (NBDA) regional conference were filmed in informal conversations. The NBDA is an advocacy organization whose annual conference in August 2007 was attended by around three hundred Black Deaf people. Informal conversations were recorded by research team members Joseph Hill and Roxanne King.

---

8. As chapter 2 notes, the Hampton school was closed in June 2008, and operations consolidated with the Virginia School for the Deaf and Blind in Staunton.

Participants

Participants at each of the six sites included members of the local Black Deaf community, selected to represent the "55 and over" and the "35 and under" general age groups. Because Deaf families are traditionally held in high esteem in the community, attempts were made to recruit them as participants, and out of seventy-six total participants for whom we have demographic data, nine are from deaf families.[9] The older participants related the history of the schools during segregation and provided a basis for contrast with the younger signers. The older signers also offered crucial information about language use in the schools and about teachers' characteristics (i.e., whether they were deaf or hearing, Black or White). The signers filmed at the NBDA conference represent a sampling of the conference attendees. The latter were not formal interviews but rather were casual conversations and narratives that were told in the course of the conversations.

Table 3.1 summarizes the available demographic information about the ninety-six signers who were filmed at the six sites and at the NBDA meeting.

Table 3.1. Participant Characteristics

	35 Years and Younger		55 Years and Older		
	F	M	F	M	Total
Alabama	2	4	5	3	14
Arkansas	3	3	5	6	17
Louisiana	1	4	4	2	11
North Carolina	3	4	4	3	14
Texas	2	1	3	2	8
Virginia	2	3	4	3	12
NBDA	0	0	14	6	20
Total	13	19	39	25	96

9. Demographic data are not available for the participants at the NBDA conference.

The Contact Persons

Following the procedures used Lucas, Bayley, and Valli (2001), the signers at each of the six sites were identified and recruited by contact persons who live in the area and with whom the participants are very familiar. These contact people were similar to the "brokers" described by Milroy, individuals who "have contacts with large numbers of individuals" in the community (1987, 70). Arranging the filming required intense communication between the first author of this book and the contact people prior to the team's arrival at the site. The contact persons played a crucial role in explaining the purpose of the filming in general terms to the participants. Even so, some reluctance to participate was evident. According to Lucas, Bayley, and Valli (2001), the source of this reluctance is twofold: (1) a fear of being video-taped because of the participants' knowledge that these videotapes will be shown outside of the community, and (2) a lack of understanding of the significance of the research. We encountered only one extreme reaction: A potential participant expressed the fear that "the Gallaudet researchers" would be "stealing our language" and that they would be profiting mone-tarily. When it was explained that the research could only benefit the Black Deaf community by documenting its history and language use, the poten-tial participant felt more comfortable, but this explanation unfortunately came only after the signer's fears had influenced a number of other potential participants not to show up for the filming after they had initially agreed to do so. In all other cases, however, the contact persons were able to respond to any concerns and recruit the number of signers needed.

Settings for the Filming

Signers were filmed in four settings. In addition, because research has shown that different genres (e.g., narrative or conversation) may result in significant differences in use of variable linguistic forms (Bayley, Lucas, and Rose 2000; Jia and Bayley 2002; Travis 2007), we collected data representing a number of different genres. First, signers participated in free conversation lasting between 30 and 40 minutes without any researchers present. Participants were asked to chat among themselves, and it was never the case that the signers lacked something to talk about. At several sites, we filmed during school reunions, and the participants were very busy catching up on news. One group was filmed following the national election on November 4, 2008. The conversation on that occasion included a long discussion about the outcome of the election and about what President Obama's name sign might be. Second, following the free conversation, the Black members of the research team conducted interviews lasting 30–40 minutes with the participants. The interviews focused on the signers' life stories, particularly their educational experience, their school, and the nature of language use both in and out of the classroom when they were students. Participants were also shown pictures of specific signs and asked what their signs were for the items in the picture. This was done to revisit specific claims about lexical variation (see chapter 8 for the results). The interview questions were as follows:

1. Tell us about your school experience:
   - Where did you go to school?
   - Where and when did you learn to sign?
   - Did/do you go to school with Black students only?
   - Were/are your teachers Black or White?
   - Were/are your teachers deaf or hearing?
   - Did/do your teachers sign? Did they sign ASL?
   - Did the Black teachers sign like Black people or like White people?

2. Do you think Black people sign differently from White people?
   - Can you explain how it's different?
   - Can you think of specific signs that are different?
   - Are there older signs that you don't see much anymore?
   - Do you sign differently with Black people than with White people? If so, how and why?
   - What are some signs that are unique to this area or to this state?

3. Do you sign differently depending on the situation—for example, in a formal situation compared to an informal situation? If so, how?

4. Do you sign differently to people of different ages? How?

Third, after completing the interviews, the researchers elicited narratives. Forty-five years of research findings about the structure of ASL provide us with a very clear picture of the language as used by White signers, including narrative conventions and narrative development (see, e.g., Galvan and Taub 2004; Rayman 1999). In order to examine possible differences between White and Black narrative styles, we completed a focused narrative elicitation: Black signers at the six sites were asked to view a portion of a wordless cartoon and then retell it to another participant. Two different cartoons were used. During the spring of 2008, twelve White signers were recruited for the same task. Chapter 6 compares the cartoon retellings of the Black signers with those of the White signers. In addition, as in Lucas, Bayley, and Valli (2001), the informal conversations and interview sections of the data contain examples of narratives of personal experience. In fact, the interview protocols were designed to elicit such narratives, particularly those dealing with the Black deaf experience. These more informal narratives provide another source of data for the analysis of Black deaf narrative style.

The fourth setting for filming was the August 2007 NBDA meeting held in St. Louis, Missouri, during which two members of the research team filmed spontaneous conversations and narratives. The conversations and interviews were filmed using two Canon GL2 digital video (DV) cameras that were positioned so as to capture the contribution of each person in the group. Following the filming, the contents of the mini-DVs were transferred to the hard drive of a video recorder, and DVD copies were made of each mini-DV. In addition, the contents of each mini-DV were summarized: We noted specific responses to the interview questions, as well as the informants' observations and use of language during the free conversation portion of the filming.

Specific Features Examined

As we state in chapter 1, there is a great deal of anecdotal evidence of a Black variety of ASL. Our main challenge in this project was to identify and to analyze the specific linguistic features that might make up this variety and to compare the use of the features in the production of Black and White signers. Based on the data and findings of Lucas, Bayley, and Valli (2001), interviews recorded at an NBDA conference, earlier research on Black ASL, and consultations with members of the Black Deaf community, we chose seven variables for analysis in the areas of phonology, syntax, discourse, and language contact. We also analyzed differences in the lexicon. Although there may well be other areas where Black and White ASL varieties differ, these seven features were the most striking in the available data. Table 3.2 summarizes the features, and we discuss them later in more detail.

Phonology

The Use of Two-Handed versus One-Handed Signs

One hand can often be deleted in two-handed signs. Woodward and DeSantis (1977) claimed that Black signers used more two-handed signs that did White signers. Tapes used in Lucas, Bayley, and Valli (2001) and recorded at the NBDA conference reveal numerous examples of signs produced with two hands by Black signers but with only one hand by White signers, such as LIE, FINE, HAPPY, and DON'T-KNOW. Recently, Lucas et al. (2007) completed a quantitative analysis of signs produced by 137 signers (84 White and 53 Black, using the data from Lucas, Bayley, and Valli 2001). Statistical analysis of 2,258 tokens shows that the Black signers in the sample were more likely than White signers to use the two-handed variants. In the current study, we sampled the free conversation and interview portions of the data tapes for examples of variation between two-handed and one-handed signs.

The Lowering of Signs Produced on the Face in Citation Form

Woodward, Erting, and Oliver (1976) claimed that White signers produced more signs on the face than did Black signers, while Lucas, Bayley, and Valli (2001) report that Black signers favor the nonlowered citation forms

Table 3.2. Features Selected for Analysis

Feature Type	Feature	Data Analyzed
phonology	variation between one-handed and two-handed signs	818 tokens from free conversations, interviews, and NBDA conversations
	location of signs such as KNOW	877 tokens from interviews and NBDA conversations
	size of the signing space in Black and White ASL	2,247 tokens from elicited and free narratives
syntax	clausal or phrasal repetition	26 ten-minute conversations
discourse and pragmatics	constructed dialogue and constructed action	24 elicited narratives; 21 free narratives
contact with English	voiceless mouthing of English	26 ten-minute conversations
contact with AAE (lexical, phrasal)	borrowing of expressions from AAE (e.g., "girl," "my bad")	examples spontaneously produced in interviews and free conversations
lexicon	differences in Black and White signs for common items and concepts (e.g., MOVIE, COLOR, RABBIT)	spontaneously produced examples, spontaneously discussed signs, and responses to specific interview questions

of signs represented by the sign KNOW, which is produced at the forehead level (citation forms are those that appear in dictionaries and are taught in sign language classes). The tapes from Lucas, Bayley, and Valli (2001) and the earlier NBDA tapes reveal examples of KNOW that are produced not only at the forehead by Black signers but also in the middle of the forehead, an older form of the sign. For this variable, as well as for variable lowering of signs such as KNOW, the free conversation and interview portions of the data tapes were sampled to provide a representative cross-section of the data.[10]

The Size of the Signing Space

Anecdotal accounts, the data from Lucas, Bayley, and Valli (2001), and the NBDA tapes repeatedly support claims by Aramburo (1989), Lewis, Palmer, and Williams (1995), and Lewis (1998) that Black ASL uses a larger signing space (i.e., the typical signing space is a rectangle that covers the area from the top of the head to the waist, from shoulder to shoulder, and a foot in front of the signer). We take into account that this feature may also require morphological and discourse explanations since the size of the signing space may be altered for emphasis or as a function of constructed action and constructed dialogue. We used the cartoon retellings by Black and White signers to control for topic. To capture the size of the signing space, a grid, adjusted for the physical characteristics of the signer, was superimposed on the video screen for each retelling, allowing us to measure the size of each signer's signing space and compare it empirically with others. Additionally, the camera was positioned the same distance from each signer to ensure comparability across signers.

The three phonological variables lend themselves to quantification and have been subjected to multivariate analysis with VARBRUL (Sankoff, Tagliamonte, and Smith 2005; Young and Bayley 1996), a specialized

---

10. While it would be ideal to code all of the data, the labor-intensive nature of coding sign language data makes such a goal unfeasible. Therefore, we have sampled randomly selected portions of the conversational and interview data.

application of the statistical procedure known as *logistical regression*, which has long been used in sociolinguistic studies of variation (Bayley 2002). With VARBRUL, the researcher can model the multiple linguistic and social factors that influence a signer's choice of one or another linguistic variant.

Syntax

Data from Lucas, Bayley, and Valli (2001) and the NBDA, as well as anecdotal reports, suggest that Black signers may use clausal or phrasal repetition more frequently than White signers, as in the following examples: HAVE SON NOW, HAVE SON ("I have a son now."); LAST-YEAR PRO.I VISIT NEW YORK, NEW YORK, NEW YORK ("I visited New York last year"). Randomly selected ten-minute clips from the current project, as well as randomly selected clips of White signers from Lucas, Bayley, and Valli (2001), were used for the analysis of repetition. The number and kind of repetitions have been counted and analyzed for form and function.

Discourse

Constructed Dialogue and Constructed Action

Constructed dialogue and constructed action (Tannen 1989; Metzger 1999) are very commonly used in ASL discourse, as signers report conversations and take the role of individuals or entities they have interacted with. An analysis by Metzger and Mather (2004), based on the data collected by Lucas, Bayley, and Valli (2001), suggests that both strategies may be used more extensively in Black than in White ASL. We have analyzed the cartoon retellings, as well as selected narratives that occurred spontaneously in the free conversation and interview data.

Mouthing of English

Data from Lucas, Bayley, and Valli (2001) and the NBDA reveal markedly less mouthing of English words by the Black signers in both narratives and conversations. Some of the interviewees showed no mouthing at all. We have analyzed bounded sections of the free conversation and interview data and compared them with the mouthing behavior of White signers.

Creation of the Corpora for the Analysis of the Size of the Signing Space, Constructed Action and Dialogue, and Mouthing

In order to analyze the size of the signing space, constructed action and dialogue, and mouthing, we created two corpora from the videotaped data. Creating the two corpora enabled us grasp the more than thirty hours of recordings by twenty-one groups of signers and six hours of filming at NBDA. Corpus 1 was created for the analyses of the size of the signing space and the use of constructed action and constructed dialogue. Equal numbers of elicited cartoon retellings were selected for Black and White signers, representing both age groups—young and old—for a total of twenty-four narratives. In addition, twenty-one free narratives (i.e., non-elicited narratives that occurred in the course of conversation) were selected, representing both Black and White signers. Black signers included representatives of all of the states in the study, while the White signers included people from Kansas, Louisiana, Maryland, Virginia, and Washington State, as well as a group of young signers recruited at Gallaudet University.

Corpus 1 allowed us to analyze and compare the use of constructed action and constructed dialogue in two different genres. We tallied the frequency of constructed action and constructed dialogue and also analyzed the nature of the constructions. That is, what kinds of events do constructed action and constructed dialogue deal with, and what kinds are simply being narrated? Are there noticeable differences between the Black signers and the White signers?

We created Corpus 2 for the analysis of clausal repetition and voiceless mouthing. From a pool of ninety-five possible video clips of ordinary conversation, we randomly selected twenty-four: twelve of Black signers from the current project (six young and six old), and twelve of White signers who were recorded in the earlier project reported in Lucas, Bayley, and Valli (2001) (also six young and six old). Signers were randomly selected so that we would not be influenced by our informal observation that Black signers use more clausal repetition and less voiceless mouthing than do White signers, an observation that would no doubt have biased our selection of clips. As in the case of Corpus 1, the Black signers represented all of the sites in the current study, while the White signers came from Kansas, Louisiana, Maryland, Massachusetts, Virginia, and Washington State.

For the analysis of clausal repetition, we tallied instances of repetition and also examined the kind of structure that was repeated. For voiceless mouthing, we tallied the frequency of mouthing and analyzed the lexical items and structures the participants were mouthing.

Contact with African American English

Anecdotal reports and informal observations attest to the outcomes of contact with AAE, in particular the use of AAE lexical items and phrases such as "My bad," "Girl!" "He my home boy," and "I ain't playin' "—either simultaneously spoken and signed (i.e., code mixing) or incorporated into Black ASL (i.e., borrowing) or spoken without signing (i.e., code switching). We have analyzed the free conversation and interview data and noted as many instances as possible. The participants produced examples naturally in conversation and also provided examples in response to the interview questions pertaining to differences between Black signing and White signing.

With the exception of the signers from Louisiana, the Black signers discussed in Lucas, Bayley, and Valli (2001) are from the North, specifically Boston, Kansas City, and Missouri, as well as from Fremont, California, so their signing provides a rich basis for comparison with the signing of the southerners in the current study. As with the earlier study, examples of the specific features were not explicitly elicited, as our focus was on language use that is as natural as possible.

Lexical Variation

In addition to the features already listed, we undertook two analyses of lexical variation: First, we analyzed the signs that were either *produced naturally* or *discussed* by the signers in the free conversation and interview portions of the data. Many examples occurred naturally, and others were produced during the interview as a result of direct questions from the researchers. However, on numerous occasions, the participants themselves initiated discussions about lexical variation during the free conversation portion of the filming. Signs were analyzed by semantic category, regional differences, and age differences. Second, at the end of the interview, we showed the participants a set of pictures to elicit signs claimed to be produced differently by Black signers and White signers in the South, specifically MOVIE, COLOR, RABBIT, PEANUT, PEACH, and LEMON (Woodward, Erting, and Oliver 1976), as well as their sign for AFRICA. The analysis reexamines this claim.

This study examined a range of variables at different linguistic levels. Hence, a variety of methods was called for. In some cases (e.g., the size of the signing space), we analyzed all of the tokens produced by a representative sample of Black and White signers engaged in particular tasks. In other cases (e.g., the lowering of signs such as KNOW), we sampled sections of the interviews and free conversations recorded at each site. In still other cases, such as the examination of mouthing of English words, we restricted the analysis to ten-minute segments randomly selected from free conversations, and we compared the new data from this study with a similar amount of data from White signers randomly selected from Lucas, Bayley, and Valli's (2001) data. This multifaceted approach to analysis has enabled us to document systematically in considerable detail the features of Black ASL that have previously been described only anecdotally.

4

Signers' Perceptions of Black ASL

While the sociohistorical foundation of Black ASL described in chapter 2 helps us understand how a separate variety of ASL might develop as a result of geographic and social factors and the analyses of specific linguistic features in chapters 5 through 8 help us define this variety in precise ways, information about users' perceptions provides insight into how people view themselves within the sociohistorical context and what they think about language use. As we will see, it is not uncommon for users' perceptions to differ from linguistic reality.

PERCEPTION OF LANGUAGE VARIETIES

Linguists define a *dialect* as a language variety that is structurally related to another variety in terms of phonological, morphological, syntactic, and semantic features regardless of its standard or stigmatized status, which is socially defined by a society (Wolfram 1991). However, the definition is not shared by the general population, whose definition of *dialect* is usually reserved for language varieties that are considered substandard in comparison with those that are socially acceptable. Language varieties with stigmatized or unfavorable linguistic features are often relegated to substandard status, and the stigmatization is always based on the social characteristics of the marginalized groups. This has been investigated

We express our gratitude to Stephanie Johnson, who contributed substantially to this chapter.

extensively. For example, in Illinois, the South Midland dialect is viewed unfavorably in comparison with the North Midland dialect because of particular linguistic features that resemble something a southerner or a farmer might use: an intrusive /r/ ("warsh" instead of "wash") and a vowel /æu/ (Frazer 1987). Southerners are generally perceived to be "informal," "undereducated," and "friendly" as reported in a language attitude study on northern and southern dialects (Preston 1996).

African American English (popularly known as Ebonics) is another example of an American dialect that is highly stigmatized. According to linguistic studies, AAE is a legitimate language variety with certain phonological, morphological, lexical, and semantic features used by African American speakers in urban and rural communities (Wolfram and Thomas 2002). Not all African Americans use AAE, nor is it exclusive to African Americans. As with any language variety, anyone who has sufficient access and exposure can acquire it. Nonetheless, the typical AAE users are African Americans.

Despite the fact that AAE has been shown to be a legitimate language variety, it is still perceived negatively in the United States in the social, mass, and entertainment media. For example, the Internet contains many sites that feature offensive parodies of AAE (Ronkin and Karn 1999), and AAE is negatively represented in entertainment, including popular Disney films (Lippi-Green 1997; Rickford and Rickford 2000). In education, the Oakland (California) School Board's decision to use AAE to teach standard English in the 1990s raised intense controversy and even outrage, particularly among people who had never paid the slightest attention to the city's educational problems (Baugh 2000; Rickford and Rickford 2000; Vaughn-Cook 2007; Winford 2003; Wolfram 1998). As a result of their dialect, some educators have viewed AAE-speaking African American children as speech impaired (Obgu 1999) and as verbally deprived (Labov 1972a). Finally, as Baugh (1996, 2000, 2003) has shown, people who speak AAE have been subject to housing discrimination. Even in the face of the adverse perception of AAE, it continues to exist because it serves as a symbol of cultural solidarity among AAE speakers. In fact, African Americans' choice of speaking mainstream English with AAE speakers may be perceived as condescending and trying to act "White" (Fordham 1999). A choice of dialect in a particular situation is much more than just speaking differently. It is a manifestation of social identity and cultural association in every community, including Deaf communities.

Deaf signers, who are also aware of and express attitudes about signing varieties in the American Deaf community (Baer, Okrent, and Rose 1996), have a perception that a standard ASL exists. The earliest recognition of a standard ASL can be traced back to 1834, when further schools for the deaf were opened after the first deaf school, the American School for the Deaf (Lane, Hoffmeister, and Bahan 1996), was founded. Graduates of the ASD were hired as teachers and served as agents of ASL dissemination, as did deaf students. Croneberg (1965) has explicitly stated that "the body of signs used at Gallaudet, then, must contain the main base of what we call standard ASL" (134).

At the opposite end of the signing spectrum is manually coded English (MCE), which belongs to a category of various English-based signed communication systems (e.g., Seeing Essential English [SEE 1], Signing Exact English [SEE 2], and Linguistics of Visual English [LOVE]). Although MCE is not a natural language as is ASL, it is still practiced in some educational settings for deaf students with the goal of developing better English skills. With written and spoken English and ASL coexisting in the community, a variety called "contact signing" (Lucas and Valli 1992) has emerged; "contact signing" utilizes features of both ASL and English (and of MCE) to varying degrees. With the use of MCE, contact signing, and ASL in the American Deaf community, issues of perception have emerged surrounding the nature of ASL.

One of the issues concerns the differences in perceptions of ASL. For example, in Lucas and Valli's (1992) study of contact signing, one clip was perceived differently by two racial groups of deaf participants. Thirty-seven percent of the White participants identified it as "ASL," while 82 percent of the Black participants identified it as "ASL" (70). This discrepancy could be based on signers' decisions to focus on different linguistic features, although we lack evidence for a definitive statement. However, we may soon have more definite evidence. This kind of discrepancy in perceptions between Black signers and White signers is being explored by Hill (forthcoming) in a large study that benefits from the statistical analysis lacking in Lucas and Valli's study. Hill is examining the linguistic and social factors that influence ASL signers' perceptions of signing across the full spectrum from ASL signing to English-like signing. The linguistic factors in Hill's study include handshape, nonmanual signals, morphemic movements, choice of signs, syntax, and prosody in signing. The social factors include age, race, and age of ASL acquisition.

Another issue is the perception of ASL and English (including SEE, lipreading, and written and spoken English) as good or bad language. Kannapell (1989) conducted a sociolinguistic study on the attitudes of deaf Gallaudet University students toward ASL and English, as well as the social factors contributing to the attitudes. She found that the pertinent social factors are the number of years spent at a Deaf school, the age of sign language acquisition, the age of onset of hearing loss, and the hearing status of parents and siblings. She also found that the students who were culturally Deaf favored ASL over English, whereas the subjects who were hard of hearing or deaf but preferred oral communication were more favorably disposed toward English and its signing forms. Students, both deaf and hard of hearing, expressed their opinions about ASL and English, which included the belief that ASL is a language but that it lacks proper grammar like English. Some students also felt that ASL has a bad effect on English skills and that while ASL is important for deaf children, speech must be taught in order for them to be able to fit in with mainstream society. Some students believed that ASL is used by less educated deaf people (Kannapell 1989, 203).

From the point of view of the scientific study of language, no language variety is better than any other in terms of linguistic structure or expressive power. It is natural for language varieties to differ from each other on numerous dimensions as a result of geographic and social factors. Social perceptions can influence the prestige of language varieties in a society, as shown in the examples of northern and southern dialects of American English, AAE, and the spectrum of signing between ASL and MCE. Black ASL is no exception, as the next section shows.

Black Deaf Signers' School History and Language Use

During the interviews, we asked the participants specific questions about their use of language, such as when they had learned to sign, the languages they used in school, the teachers' signing skills, older signs that were unique to school and region, and their perception of the difference between Black and White signing.[11] Table 4.1 shows the number of responses to the questions about where they had learned to sign and how.

Most of the signers, regardless of age, learned to sign at school. Eleven older signers reported that they learned directly from their teachers while ten older signers reported that they learned from teachers and classmates. Four

Table 4.1. Signers' ASL Acquisition

where they learned signs	55 and Older	35 and Younger
at school	36	21
at home	1	6
at both	1	2
how they learned signs		
teachers only	11	0
teachers and classmates	10	5
socializing with classmates	3	9
school resources (flashcards, interpreters, books)	4	1
deaf family	2	5
nondeaf family	0	1
other deaf adult (nonfamily)	2	1

11. In tables 4.1–4.4, the number of responses may not add up to the total number of signers. Participants were interviewed in groups, so if their fellow signers were alumni of the same school and had already answered the questions, they might not have answered.

Table 4.2. Race of Students at Signers' Former Schools

School Demography	55 and Older	35 and Younger
only Black	38	0
mostly Black	2	0
only Black, then mixed	0	4
mixed	0	26
mostly White	1	2

older signers said that they learned to sign from other sources, such as flashcards and books. Only two signers had Deaf language models to learn from.

Younger signers who learned to sign at school also learned from teachers and classmates. One young signer mentioned an interpreter as a language model. Younger signers who learned at home acquired sign language from Deaf families, but one signer reported that a hearing family member was a language model.

Table 4.2 shows the number of responses to the question about the racial demography of the students at school.

As table 4.2 shows, 40 out of 41 older signers reported that their schools had only or mostly Black students. This was expected because the schools were segregated. One older signer, however, attended a White school. In contrast, most younger signers attended racially integrated schools. Four younger signers reported that they were racially segregated at first and then were allowed to be in racially mixed environments with their White peers. Two younger signers reported that they went to school with mostly White students.

Table 4.3 summarizes responses to the questions about racial identity and the hearing or Deaf identity of teachers.

Most older signers reported that they had only Black or mostly Black teachers, but seven older signers had only White or mostly White teachers. Seven signers reported that they had only White teachers and later had both Black and White teachers. Also, many participants reported that they had hearing teachers, and nine (seven from the older group and two from the younger group) had Deaf teachers.

Table 4.3. Teachers' Identities at Signers' Former Schools

Race of teachers	55 and Older	35 and Younger
Black	20	0
most Black	5	0
both	0	12
most White	1	9
White	6	6
Black at one school, White at another	0	6
White at beginning, then mixed	7	0
deaf or hearing teachers		
deaf	7	2
most deaf	2	1
both	0	5
most hearing	2	12
most hearing, but then moved to school with both	0	2
hearing	23	8

As expected, some younger signers had Black and White teachers, while other signers had only White or mostly White teachers. Like the older signers, most had hearing teachers. Seven signers had both hearing and deaf teachers (five reported "both," two reported "most deaf," and two reported "most hearing but then moved to school with both").

Table 4.4 summarizes the comments from participants about their teachers' signing skills.

A few of the younger and older signers had teachers who were skillful in ASL, but most of the signers reported that their teachers were not signing ASL. Some signers said that their teachers communicated by fingerspelling, and others said that their teachers signed in SEE. Also, some of the signers said that their teachers were not skilled in signing.

Table 4.4. Signers' Comments about Teachers' Signing Skills

Teachers' signing	55 and Older	35 and Younger
Mostly fingerspelling	2	3
Unskilled signing	8	9
Basic signing, simultaneous communication, total communication	3	2
Signed Exact English	11	7
ASL	8	4
Some of everything	0	4
Comparison of Black and White teachers' signing		
The signing is different.	14	19
The signing is similar.	0	1
Undecided	0	2

Later in the interviews, the participants responded to a few questions about the difference between Black and White signing. Forty-six signers, divided equally between the two age groups, responded to these questions. Overwhelmingly, they said that Black signing differs from White signing. Only one signer (from the younger group) said that Black signing and White signing are similar.

BLACK DEAF SIGNERS' PERCEPTIONS OF BLACK ASL

The signers' interview responses were very rich. Here we describe a number of themes that emerged from them.

"White Deaf Education Is Better."

A common statement from the older signers was that their own school was inferior to White deaf schools. They said that their schools had fewer recreational activities, sports, and materials than White schools and that their own teachers' signing skills were not as good. They also complained that they did not learn much at school. Some older signers who transferred to White schools reported that the school materials and assignments were much more difficult than the ones they had in the Black deaf schools. Also, the signers who transferred reported that White teachers' signing was so different from their own they could not understand it, and they assumed that the signing was better because it was more complex and had a more extensive vocabulary.

Even long after court-ordered desegregation following the 1954 case of *Brown vs. Board of Education,* some younger signers complained about the quality of education in their racially mixed schools, which had formerly been segregated. For example, one Virginia group had a long discussion about education at their school in Hampton. They felt that the Hampton school was not as good as the Model Secondary School for the Deaf (MSSD) in Washington, D.C., where they later transferred. One important difference was that they did not say that White deaf education was better; however, even though the formerly segregated school had been desegregated, in their opinion the quality of education there had not improved.

"White Signing Is Better and More Advanced."

Most older signers said that White signing was better because it differed in vocabulary and complexity. One signer from Louisiana said that White signing was better because "it was difficult to understand." She was not the only person with that sentiment. Many other older signers shared this perception as well, which might be related to their perception of education: If it was challenging, then it must be superior. One Texas signer expressed the opinion that Black signing was "more gestural" and White signing was "cleaner," but she added that Black deaf people were not ashamed of their language. The last statement was striking because all of the signers seemed willing to set aside their signing to adopt White signing; in fact, many of the older signs that they had used at the segregated school were no longer in use.

A few of the younger signers believed that White signing was better than Black signing, but not for the same reasons given by the older signers. One young participant from Louisiana said that White signing was better than Black signing because Black signing had a thuggish or "street" component that would be inappropriate in some settings (e.g., WHAT'S-UP NIGGA?) However, another Louisiana signer disagreed and said that *both* Black and White signing—not just Black signing—had proper and improper forms. Most younger signers held a positive discussion about Black signing, which leads to the third theme.

"Black Signing Is Different from White Signing Based on Style, Attitude, and Culture."

While both older and younger signers agreed that Black signing is different from White signing, the younger signers offered more positive comments about the former. A group of signers from Texas said that Black signing was more powerful in expression and movement and that it had rhythm and style, whereas White signing was more monotonic and lacking in emotion—"not fun to watch," as one of them mentioned. Also, this group said that Black deaf signers were able to show their true selves in their signing and that White signers were snobbish. It may seem that this group was critical of White signing, but one member did say that White signing was polite and courteous in comparison to Black signing.

One North Carolina signer made an interesting observation about ASL discourse. According to her, Black deaf people do not maintain eye contact with signers during a conversation. In general, eye contact is an important discourse function to maintain in a conversation between ASL signers, and breaking eye contact is considered impolite. Another North Carolina signer remarked that Black deaf signers tried to behave like Black hearing people with similar manners and expressions.

"Younger Black Deaf Signers Sign Differently Depending on Situation and People."

Younger signers showed an awareness of diversity in signing styles and said that they changed their register depending on the situation and the social characteristics of their interlocutors. One signer from Louisiana observed that when he socialized with older Black deaf signers, he knew that they signed differently, so he tried to accommodate to their signing; when he was with his peers, he signed like them. One Texan said that when she was at school or work, she was signing "White" to give a professional appearance (as opposed to signing "Black," which was more "street," as one Virginian remarked). A group of signers from Virginia commented that the signing at their school in Hampton was more uniform than that at the Model Secondary School for the Deaf.

In conclusion, both older and younger signers agreed that a difference exists between Black signing and White signing, but they offered divergent reasons for the variation. Older signers held a negative view of Black signing because of their experience in segregated schools, where fewer activities and resources were available and their teachers had poor signing and teaching skills. Younger signers held a more positive view of Black signing as a result of their increased metalinguistic awareness and positive Black cultural expressions, but they said that Black signing was more "street" compared to White signing, which was polite and courteous (i.e., more standard). In the following chapters, our linguistic analyses show that, in contrast to these perceptions, Black ASL has some linguistic features that conform more closely to standard, prescriptive forms of ASL than does White signing.

5

Phonological Variation

In this chapter we examine three variable features of Black ASL: signs that can be produced with one or two hands, the location of signs such as KNOW, which is usually produced on the forehead but is sometimes made at a lower level, and the size of the signing space. All three variables have been explored in ASL (Aramburo 1989; Lewis, Palmer, and Williams 1995; Lucas et al. 2007; Lucas, Bayley, and Valli 2001; Lucas et al. 2002; Mauk and Tyrone 2008) and, in the case of the lowering of signs such as KNOW, in Australian and New Zealand sign languages as well (Schembri et al. 2009). In addition, anecdotal accounts suggest that Black and White ASL differ in their use of these features. However, no large-scale studies have yet documented those differences. In the following sections, we report on a series of quantitative analyses of the three variables, based on data from the signers examined in this project. For each variable, we first summarize the results of previous research. We then present the quantitative results for the Black ASL data and, where possible, compare them with previous studies. Finally, we discuss the implications for the nature of Black ASL as a dialect of ASL.

HANDEDNESS

Previous Research

One critical difference between spoken and sign languages that directly affects patterns of variation is that spoken languages use only one articulator

---

We gratefully acknowledge Anika Stephen's substantial contribution to this chapter.

during production (given that humans have only one vocal apparatus), while sign languages use two (the two hands). As Brentari (1998) observes:

> Two-handed signs are so intriguing to phonologists who are interested in sign languages because they provide such a clear case of a phonetic difference between signed and spoken languages. . . . The phonetic difference lies in the fact that spoken languages do not have two identical articulators of any sort that could behave in the way that the two hands behave in sign. (247)

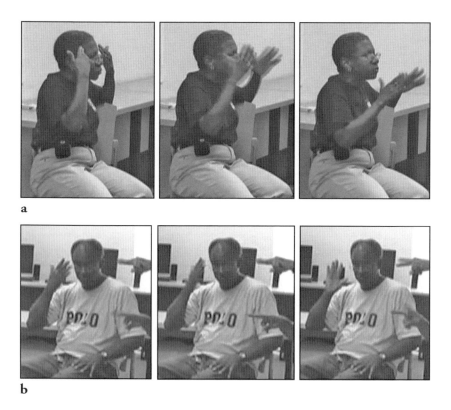

Figures 5.1a and 5.1b. Two-handed and one-handed variants of DON'T-KNOW.

That is, some two-handed lexical items can be produced with only one hand without detracting from their meaning, while producing other two-handed signs with only one hand may cause misunderstanding. Examples of signs that may be produced with one or two hands include DEER, WANT, STILL, NOW, LIVE, and DON'T-KNOW. Figures 5.1a and 5.1b illustrate the one-handed and two-handed variants of DON'T-KNOW.

The production of two-handed signs with only one hand is often viewed as a more casual type of signing; thus, two-handed signs tend to be used in more formal discourse. As well, many signers believe that the choice between a one- or two-handed variant is quite random; there appears to be no particular reason to choose one over the other. In this section we examine such variation and pay particular attention to the specific influences, both linguistic and social, that contribute to the one-handed production of these two-handed signs.

Battison (1974, 1978) first examined two-handed signs in depth. Starting with a 1974 paper in *Sign Language Studies* and continuing in a 1978 book, Battison divided two-handed signs into three types. In Type 1, the hands have identical handshapes and perform identical motor acts. Their movement may be synchronous or alternating. Examples include WANT, STILL, and NOW. In Type 2 signs, the handshapes are identical, but one hand is active while the other is passive. Examples include SCHOOL, WORK, and PAPER. In type 3 signs, one hand is still active while the other is passive, and the handshapes differ, as in DISCUSS, ROUGH, and WEEK. Battison elaborates on two morpheme structure conditions, the symmetry condition and the dominance condition:

> The Symmetry Condition holds that if both hands move independently during a given two-handed sign (as opposed to one or both being static), then the specifications for handshape and movement must be identical. . . . The Dominance Condition is an implicational statement which works from the other direction. For those signs which have *non-identical* handshapes, one hand must remain static, while the other, usually the dominant one, executes the movement. (1974, 5-6)

Directly relevant to our study is which type of sign permits the deletion of one hand. Regarding this question, Battison states the following:

> Of these three types of signs, we can match the hierarchy of symmetry with the hierarchy of deletion. Those signs which do not have identical handshapes [Type 3] resist deletion of either hand, with a few exceptions of the static B (flat palm) hand mentioned earlier, which suggest that it may constitute the simplest hand contact. Those which have identical handshapes but in which only one hand moves [Type 2] sometimes allow deletion of the stationary hand, but contact is usually maintained and is realized as contact on some part of the body or on an object. Deletion is most common in signs which have the highest degree of symmetry-those with symmetrical handshapes, locations and movements [Type 1]. . . . Symmetry reduces the complexity of signs and creates much redundancy in the signal. (11)

In another early study, Frishberg (1975) conducted a diachronic analysis of the historical development of ASL signs that suggested that "signs which were previously made in contact with the face using two hands now use one" (703). This analysis implies that signers who use an older dialect would be more likely to use two-handed variants than those who use a newer dialect. More recently, Padden and Perlmutter (1987) described "weak drop" as a process whereby a two-handed sign becomes one handed and argued that the phenomenon could be explained within the framework of lexical phonology. Within the framework of prosodic phonology, Brentari (1998) explains in detail why some signs permit weak drop while others do not. She expands upon Battison's three sign types and their behavior with respect to deletion. However, although valuable, the details of Brentari's analysis are not directly relevant to the current inquiry.

With specific relevance to differences between Black and White signers, Woodward and DeSantis (1977) also examined one-handed variants of two-handed signs, though they focused on a smaller set of signs produced on the face. The goal of their analysis was to compare ASL with French Sign Language (FSL) in order to identify a direction and rate of change from two-handed to one-handed cognates in the two languages. They elicited data from 40 White Deaf signers (16 over age 47; 24 under age 47) and 35 African American Deaf signers (33 over age 47; 2 under age 47). Signers were asked to supply their signs for CAT, CHINESE, COW, DEER, and DONKEY. Results indicated that factors affecting whether the variant would be one or two handed were the outward movement of the sign, whether the location at which it was produced on the face was high or low, and complex movements of the target sign. In addition, Woodward and DeSantis suggested that change in two-handed signs was affected by various social factors, among them age, race, and home location. They found that southerners supplied more two-handed variants than nonsoutherners, older White signers supplied more two-handed variants than younger White signers, and African American signers produced a greater number of two-handed signs than White signers from the same age group.

Although the varieties of ASL used by African Americans and the alternation between two-handed and one-handed variants of different signs received some attention in early research, that investigation left a number of questions unanswered. Questions related to linguistic constraints include the possible role of a sign's grammatical function in conditioning the variation, as well as the importance of assimilation to the preceding or following signs. Questions about social conditioning include whether the use of two-handed variants is more common in some parts of the country than in others, whether the change that Frishberg (1975) observed is continuing (i.e., younger signers used more one-handed variants than older signers), and whether African Americans continue to favor twohanded variants. Battison (1974) mentions the psychological and social variables related to deletion and tells "whether the signer was deaf or not, whether the parents were deaf, the age of onset of deafness, age of acquisition of sign language, sex, age, etc." but goes on to say that "none of the above variables have been taken into account" (8).

Lucas et al. (2007) address several of these questions, based on data collected in the mid-1990s in four regions of the United States: California,

Louisiana, Kansas/Missouri, and Massachusetts (see Lucas, Bayley, and Valli 2001 for a full account of the data and the signers' social characteristics). Using a multivariate analysis of more than 2,250 tokens from 127 African American and White signers, they found that the choice between a one-handed and a two-handed variant was constrained by a rich array of linguistic and social factors. Overall, signers used the one-handed variant at a rate of 47 percent. The one-handed variant was favored when the preceding or following sign was also one handed and when there was a preceding or following pause. In addition, the one-handed variant was favored when the target sign contacted the face or the body. Furthermore, nouns, verbs, adjectives, and adverbs disfavored the one-handed variant, whereas *wh*-signs and a number of other function words and interjections (e.g., WOW) favored it. In contrast to results reported for other variables in Lucas, Bayley, and Valli (2001), grammatical category was a rather weak constraint. The results for the social constraints are particularly relevant to the current inquiry because Lucas et al. (2007) included a small number of southern African American signers, all of whom were from Louisiana. Results showed that signers from Massachusetts and those under 55 favored the one-handed variant. Interestingly, African American signers favored the older two-handed form, which they used at a rate of 56 percent, while White signers used the one-handed variant at a rate of 50 percent.

One-Handed vs. Two-Handed Signs in Southern Black ASL

In this section we address the following questions:

1. Do southern Black signers favor two-handed signs in comparison to White signers or Black signers in other areas of the United States?
2. Do older southern Black signers favor two-handed signs in comparison to younger Black signers in the same region?
3. What are the linguistic constraints on the production of two-handed vs. one-handed signs?
4. What are the social constraints on the production of two-handed vs. one-handed signs?

The Envelope of Variation

A sociolinguistic variable may be defined as two ways of saying (or signing) the same thing, with the distribution of different forms influenced by linguistic and social factors (Labov 1972b). For example, an ASL user may sign DEAF from ear to chin or from chin to ear. However, the meaning does not change. Moreover, as Bayley, Lucas, and Rose (2000) have shown, signers' choices among the different forms of DEAF are affected by the grammatical class to which the sign belongs, as well as by a number of social factors, including the region where the signer lives and the signer's age. Turning to another example of such variation, it is clear that DEER signed with two hands and DEER signed with one hand refer to the same creature.

Before we begin coding examples, then, we first need to decide which signs to include in the envelope of variation and which ones to exclude. In the present case, the task is complicated to a certain extent by the fact that ASL contains different types of two-handed signs. Recall that signs of Type 1 can be produced with only one articulator (e.g., DEER, DON'T KNOW, FINISH, HORSE, NOW, PONDER, SICK, TIRED, WANT). Signs of Type 2 may be divided into two subtypes. Type 2a signs cannot as a rule be produced with only one hand (e.g., CAN'T, CHEESE, CHURCH, SOCKS, STAR, WORK). Signs that we have designated as Type 2b (e.g., RIGHT, PAPER, SCHOOL, SHOES) can be produced with a substitute base or with one hand in very particular discourse situations. For the present study, we coded only signs that can be produced with two hands or one hand unremarkably. Signs of Type 2 (both subtypes) were excluded as being either outside the "envelope of variation" or subject to constraints that have nothing to do with linguistic variation, such as the presence or absence of a convenient substitute base.

Coding and Analysis for Handedness

Guided by previous claims, as well as the earlier study of Lucas et al. (2007), we coded more than eight hundred signs drawn from interviews and free conversations to test the following possible constraints on the signers' choice between the one-handed and two-handed variants of Type 1 signs:

1. dependent variable: one-handed, two-handed
2. contact (or not) with the face or the body
3. handedness of preceding sign: one-handed, two-handed, pause
4. handedness of following sign: one-handed, two-handed, pause
5. grammatical category: noun, verb, adjective, adverb, other
6. state: Alabama, Arkansas, Louisiana, North Carolina, Texas, Virginia
7. signer's gender
8. age: 35 and younger; 55 and older
9. kind of school attended: segregated, integrated, mixed (first segregated, then integrated)

Data were subjected to multivariate analysis with VARBRUL, the most commonly used program for quantitative analysis in sociolinguistics (Bayley 2002; Tagliamonte 2006).

Results

The results of VARBRUL analysis show that Black southerners' choice between one-handed and two-handed variants of Type 1 signs is systematic and constrained by both linguistic and social factors. Table 5.1 shows the results for the factors that reached statistical significance (α = .05). Note that the VARBRUL weights, or factor values, need to be interpreted in relation to the input value (i.e., the overall likelihood that a signer will choose the value selected as the application value). Factor values, or weights, between .5 and 1.0 are said to favor the application value; weights between 0 and .5 are said to disfavor the application value (the one-handed variant in the present case). Grammatical category, state, and gender failed to reach statistical significance, while the type of school the signers attended overlapped almost completely with age. As we have seen, signers aged 55 and over attended segregated schools, while those who were 35 and younger attended integrated residential or mainstream schools.

As the results in table 5.1 show, the features of the preceding and following signs condition signers' choices between one-handed and

Table 5.1. Two-Handed vs. One-Handed Signs (Application Value = One-Handed)

Factor Group	Factor	N	Percentage 1 Hand	Weight	Range
following sign	1 handed	256	45.3	.598	
	pause	288	33.0	.492	
	2 handed	274	26.6	.416	.182
preceding sign	pause or 1 handed	565	49.6	.554	
	2 handed	253	23.7	.381	.173
contact	contact	286	44.8	.603	
	no contact	532	29.3	.444	.159
age	35 and younger	349	39.5	.552	
	55 and older	469	31.1	.461	.091
Total	input	818	34.7	.336	

Note: Log likelihood = −497.783, chi-square/cell = 0.9063. Factors that did not differ significantly from one another have been combined where appropriate.

two-handed variants. If the preceding or following sign is also produced with two hands, the two-handed variant is more likely to be chosen. However, if the preceding or following sign is produced with one hand, signers tend to choose the one-handed variant. In addition, in accord with the results reported by Woodward and DeSantis (1977) and Lucas et al. (2007), contact of the target sign with the face or the body favors the one-handed form, although this constraint is not as strong as the preceding and following environment. In addition, older signers who attended segregated schools are less likely to choose the one-handed variant than younger signers who attended school after integration. Note, however, that even in environments that favor the use of the one-handed variant, use of the innovative one-handed form does not exceed 50 percent.

The results reported here differ in one important respect from many of the previous studies of phonological variation in ASL (Lucas and Bayley 2005, 2010) in that grammatical function did not reach statistical significance. Hence, it is not included in the results presented in table 5.1. The results also contrast with the results reported in Lucas et al. (2007). That study, however, was based on a much larger data set (2,258 tokens vs. 818 tokens in the present study); moreover, in Lucas et al. (2007), grammatical function was the least important of the linguistic constraints. Although we would like to offer a definite explanation for the lack of statistical significance in the present study of handedness, for now we must be content with two possibilities. First, as a relatively weak constraint, grammatical function may reach significance only when more data are included. Alternately, previous studies of phonological variation in ASL dealt with different parameters (e.g., location, handshape). It may be that the number of articulators (two hands vs. one) is dealt with differently from other parameters and is more susceptible to assimilation.

Turning to the social constraints, we find that only age (and, by implication, type of school attended) has a significant effect. Older signers who attended segregated schools are more likely to use the two-handed variants. Younger signers, who attended school after integration, are more likely to use the one-handed variant. In addition, a comparison of the results of this study with those in Lucas et al. (2007) illustrates two general trends. First, younger signers, regardless of their ethnicity or area of residence, tend to use more one-handed variants than their elders with similar social characteristics, with only one exception: northern African Americans, among whom the percentages of one-handed and two-handed variants differ only slightly. Table 5.2 and figure 5.2 compare percentages of one-handed signs from four groups of signers divided by age group: the southern African Americans in the present study; African Americans in Louisiana; African Americans in California, Massachusetts, and Missouri; White signers in California, Louisiana, Massachusetts, and Kansas. In each case, the younger African Americans use fewer one-handed variants than the younger White

Table 5.2. One-Handed vs. Two-Handed Signs: Comparison of
Results for Southern Black ASL, Louisiana Black ASL,
Northern Black ASL, and White ASL (% One-Handed)

Study	Tokens	Younger	Older	Total
southern Black ASL	818	40	31	35
Louisiana Black ASL	258	43	24	39
northern Black ASL (three sites)	855	46	44	45
White ASL (four sites)	1,145	57	37	50

Note: Data for northern Black ASL, Louisiana Black ASL, and White ASL are from Lucas et al. (2007). Data from White signers were collected in California, Kansas, Louisiana, and Massachusetts. Data from northern African Americans were collected in California, Massachusetts, and Missouri. The younger signers in Lucas et al. (2007) are age 54 and younger. Younger southern Black signers are 35 and younger. Older signers in all studies are 55+.

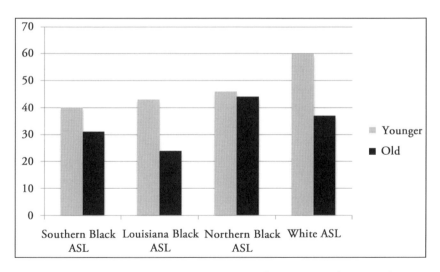

Figure 5.2. One-handed vs. two-handed signs: Comparison of results for one-handed signs in southern Black ASL, Louisiana Black ASL, northern Black ASL, and White ASL.

Table 5.3. One-Handed vs. Two-Handed Signs by State and Race

California Ethnicity	% 1H	Louisiana Ethnicity	% 1H	Kansas/ Missouri Ethnicity	% 1H	Massachusetts Ethnicity	% 1H
AA	42	AA	39	AA	38	AA	56
W	47	W	42	W	50	W	61
Total	44		40		45		59

Note: n = 2,258 (Lucas et al. 2007)

signers, who use the one-handed variant in 60 percent of the tokens. The older White signers, however, use fewer one-handed variants (37 percent) than the northern Black signers. However, the older White signers use a higher percentage of one-handed variants than the older Black signers in Louisiana studied by Lucas, Bayley, and Valli (2001) or the southern Black signers in the current study.

The results for handedness illustrate the generally conservative nature of Black ASL. The more conservative-or "standard"-nature of the ASL that African American Deaf people use is also illustrated when we break down the results from Lucas et al. (2007) by state and ethnicity (table 5.3). Although the differences are small in some states (e.g., California, Louisiana), in every case White signers use a higher percentage of one-handed signs than African Americans in the same region. We will return to the implications of these results and consider them together with the results of the quantitative analysis of our other phonological variables, the location of signs such as KNOW and the size of the signing space.

LOCATION

Location is one of the parameters that characterize signs. The signs of the class that we examine here, of which KNOW is a typical example, share features of location and hand placement. In citation, or dictionary, form (+cf), signs of this class are produced at the forehead or temple. In addition to KNOW, examples include verbs of perception and thinking (e.g., BELIEVE, DECIDE, FORGET, REMEMBER, SUPPOSE, SUSPECT, SEE, THINK), nouns (e.g., DEER, FATHER, HORSE, MOTHER, PARENT), prepositions (e.g., FOR), and interrogatives (e.g., WHY). Figure 5.3a shows TEACHER in its citation (nonlowered) form. Figure 5.3b shows the same sign in its lowered form.

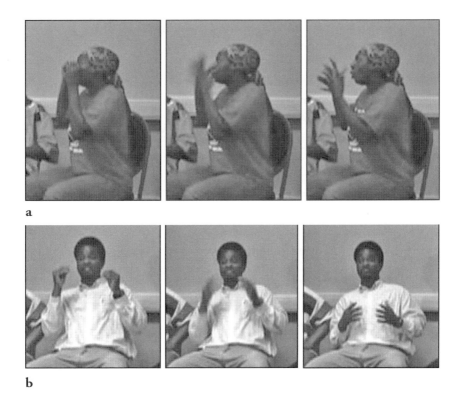

a

b

Figures 5.3a and 5.3b. TEACHER in citation and lowered form.

Previous Research on Location

Sign linguists have long recognized that signs such as KNOW can "move down" not only in ASL but in Australian (Auslan) and New Zealand Sign Languages (NZSL) as well (Frishberg 1975; Schembri et al. 2009).[12] Variants of signs such as KNOW are often produced at locations that are lower than the forehead or the temple. Liddell and Johnson comment:

> Many signs that are produced with contact at the SFH [side of forehead] location in formal signing may be produced in casual signing at the CK [check] location. . . . These same signs also appear at times without contact in the area immediately in front of the iNK [ipsilateral neck] location . . . the phonological processes that originally must have moved them are still active in contemporary ASL. (1989, 253)

The first large-scale investigation of variation in the location of signs such as KNOW was carried out by Lucas, Bayley, and Valli (2001; Lucas, Bayley, Rose, and Wulf 2002). That study examined 2,594 examples of signs of this class. Data were drawn from sociolinguistic interviews with 207 African American and White signers in seven different regions of the United States. Overall, the results indicated that signers chose the -cf, or lowered, variant slightly more than half of the time, at a rate of 53 percent. The variation was not random, however. Rather, multivariate analysis showed that lowering of signs of this class was constrained by a range of linguistic and social factors. Among the linguistic factors, the grammatical category was the strongest constraint. Nouns, verbs, and adjectives disfavored the lowered forms, while prepositions and interrogatives favored them. The location of the preceding sign also had a significant effect on signers' choices between lowered and nonlowered variants and suggested that progressive assimilation

---

12. The comparison with Auslan and NZSL provides an interesting example of a widespread process in sign languages. These two languages are closely related to one another inasmuch as they both have descended from British Sign Language. They are not related to ASL.

was at work. If the preceding sign was at the location of the body, signers were more likely to choose a lowered variant. If the preceding sign was at head level, signers were more likely to choose +cf. Finally, whether the following sign contacted the head or the body also had a significant effect. When there was no contact, lowered forms were favored. When the following sign involved contact, lowered forms were disfavored.

Social factors also played an important role in the variation. Lucas, Bayley, and Valli (2001) reported that age, gender, language background, region, ethnicity, and social class all reached statistical significance. As expected, the youngest signers, ranging in age from 15 to 24 when the data were collected in the mid-1990s, favored the -cf lowered form. Men also favored the lowered form, while signers in Washington State and Virginia disfavored it. The results for ethnicity and class are particularly relevant for the current study. Both working-class and middle-class White signers slightly favored the lowered forms, while middle-class Black signers slightly disfavored them. Working-class Black signers strongly disfavored the lowered forms.

As we have noted, the variable lowering of signs that are produced at the forehead in citation form has also been studied in Auslan and NZSL. In a recent article, Schembri et al. (2009) report on an extensive study of variation in the location parameter in the two closely related languages. Their results are summarized in table 5.4.

As in ASL, variation in location in a similar class of signs in Auslan and NZSL is constrained by a complex array of social and linguistic factors, although citation forms are more common in both Auslan and NZSL than in ASL. In all three languages, we see the influence of assimilatory processes in the influence of the preceding and following signs. Nevertheless, as one might expect when dealing with different languages, the details differ. In addition, as in ASL, grammatical category influences variation in both Auslan and NZSL, although the influence of grammatical category interacts with lexical frequency in the sign languages of the southern hemisphere. Of particular interest for the current study are the results for age in Auslan and ethnicity in NZSL. Just as in ASL, younger Auslan signers are less likely to use citation forms than their elders. Moreover, in NZSL, minority signers, in this case Maori, are less likely to use noncitation forms than deaf New Zealanders of European descent.

Table 5.4. Location Variation in Auslan and New Zealand Sign Language (NZSL) (Source: Schembri et al. 2009)

Factor	Auslan (n = 2,667)	NZSL (n = 2,096)
Linguistic constraints		
grammatical category	highly frequent verbs > others	high-frequency verbs > low-frequency
X frequency		verbs > low-frequency nouns/adj > high-frequency nouns/adj
preceding location	body > head	body > head
following location	body > head	body > head
following sign or pause	pause > sign	pause > sign
preceding contact with head, hands, or body	head or hands > no contact > body	no contact > contact
Social constraints		
age	51 or younger > older than 51	ns
region	Sydney/Melbourne > Adelaide/ Brisbane/Perth	North > South
gender	female > male	female > male
ethnicity	not tested	Pakeha (European) > Maori
language background	ns	native NZSL > middle childhood acquisition > early acquisition
language background		native signer > early childhood acquirer > middle childhood acquirer
percentage –cf	45	43
input (corrected mean)	.427	.412

"Not significant" is abbreviated as "ns."

To summarize, studies of three different sign languages, including ASL, have shown that the lowering of signs produced at the forehead in citation form is systematic and subject to complex linguistic and social constraints. This work provided the basis for our analysis of lowering in Black ASL.

Coding and Analysis for Location (Lowering)

On the basis of previous research, we formulated the following research questions:

1. Do southern Black signers favor +cf variants of signs such as KNOW in comparison to White signers or Black signers in other areas of the United States?
2. Do older southern Black signers favor +cf variants of signs such as KNOW in comparison to younger Black signers in the same region?
3. What are the linguistic constraints on the lowering of signs of this class?
4. What are the social constraints on the lowering of signs of this class?

We coded 877 tokens extracted from sociolinguistic interviews for the following linguistic factors:

1. dependent variable: +cf, -cf (lowered)
2. grammatical category: noun, verb, adjective, compound, preposition/ interrogative
3. preceding event: hold, sign, pause
4. following event: hold, sign, pause
5. location of the preceding sign: head, body
6. location of the following sign: head, body
7. preceding contact: contact with head or body (or not)
8. following contact: contact with head or body (or not)

The data were also coded for the same social factors as those in the analysis of variation between one-handed and two-handed signs, namely age, gender, state, and type of school attended. A sign was coded as a citation form (+cf) if it was produced no lower than the eyebrow ridge. It was coded as a noncitation form if it was produced lower than the eyebrow ridge.

As in the case of one-handed and two-handed signs, the data were analyzed with VARBRUL. Several combinations of factors were run to achieve the most parsimonious model that accounted for the data and to eliminate nonsignificant factors.

Results for Location (Lowering)

In contrast to the results reported for this variable in Lucas, Bayley, and Valli (2001), noncitation forms constituted a relatively small proportion of the total, only 29.2 percent. Table 5.5 shows the VARBRUL results for the linguistic factors. In interpreting the results, recall that the weight (favoring or disfavoring) needs to be interpreted in light of the input value, or the overall likelihood that a signer will choose a -cf form. For example, compounds, with a weight of .716, are said to favor -cf because signers select the lowered form at a higher rate than the overall input, or corrected mean, of .26.

As in the earlier study, the grammatical category to which a sign belongs is the most important linguistic constraint. As noted, compounds favor -cf (.716), as do nouns (.602) and prepositions or interrogatives (.582). Verbs, which constitute the majority of tokens, disfavor -cf (.448).

Whether the preceding sign contacts the head or the body also significantly affects the observed variation. When the preceding sign contacts the body, a signer is more likely to choose the lowered variant (.562). When the preceding sign is at the level of the head with no contact, a signer is less likely to choose -cf (.379). The factor weights when the preceding sign has no contact with the body (.505) or contact with the head (.492) cover the great majority of tokens and constitute nearly neutral reference points.

As table 5.6 shows, social factors also significantly affect a signer's choice of the citation form or a lowered variant. In comparison to African Americans in other states, signers in Texas favor the use of the lowered variant, using it 43.6 percent of the time (.650). Signers in Arkansas and Louisiana are the most likely to select the citation form. As table 5.6 shows, signers in these two states used the lowered variant only 23 percent of the time, for a factor weight of .405. Signers in the other three states—Alabama, North Carolina, and Virginia—were in the middle, with a weight of .529.

Age also significantly affected the choice between the two variants in the expected direction. Younger signers, who attended school after integration, were more likely to select a noncitation form (.587) than older signers who had attended segregated schools (.430). Finally, as in the results for one-handed vs. two-handed signs, gender did not reach statistical significance at the .05 level.

Table 5.5. Location: Linguistic Constraints (Application Value = –cf, Lowered Variant)

Factor Group	Factor	N	Percentage	Weight	Range
grammatical category	compound	47	48.9	.716	
	noun	111	39.6	.602	
	preposition/ interrog.	107	35.3	.582	
	adjective/adverb	60	21.7	.464	
	verb	552	25.0	.448	.268
preceding contact	body, contact	150	29.3	.562	
	body, no contact	419	27.7	.505	
	head, contact	106	26.4	.492	
	head, no contact	54	22.2	.379	.183
Total	input	877	29.2	.260	

Note: Log likelihood = –496.154, chi-square/cell = 0.9314.

Table 5.6. Location: Social Constraints (Application Value = –cf, Lowered Variant)

Factor Group	Factor	N	Percentage	Weight	Range
state	Texas	140	43.6	.650	
	Alabama, North Carolina, Virginia	454	28.6	.529	
	Arkansas, Louisiana	283	23.0	.405	.245
age	35 and younger	390	36.4	.587	
	55 and older	487	23.4	.430	.157
Total	input	877	29.2	.260	

Note: Log likelihood = –496.154, chi-square/cell = 0.9314. Factors that did not differ significantly from each other have been combined where appropriate.

The results in tables 5.5 and 5.6 are in general agreement with those reported for the location variable in Lucas, Bayley, and Valli (2001). However, there are a number of differences. First, although grammatical function is the most important linguistic constraint in both studies, the order of factors differs. In the earlier study, nouns and verbs, the vast majority of the tokens, did not differ in their effect. As we have seen, in the current study, nouns favor -cf, while verbs disfavor it. Moreover, the difference in factor weights is significant. In addition, Lucas, Bayley, and Valli (2001) report that contact of the following sign with the head or the body influenced the location of the target sign, as did the location of the preceding segment. In the current study, however, contact of the preceding sign with the head or the body proved to have a significant effect. Neither the location nor the contact of the following sign with the head or the body reached statistical significance. Finally, in Lucas, Bayley, and Valli (2001), signer gender was statistically significant, as was the language background of the signer (hearing, nonsigning parents or deaf parents).

These differences can be attributed to a number of sources. First, the dataset for the present study, in terms of both number of signers and tokens, is considerably smaller than the dataset used in the earlier study of this variable (887 tokens vs. 2,594 tokens). While the number of tokens in the current study is certainly sufficient to capture the main effects, more subtle effects might well require additional data. This is especially true in the case of factors that are relatively rare, such as compounds, with only 47 tokens, or adjectives and adverbs, with only 60 tokens combined. Of course, since Black and White signers formed separate communities and seldom interacted, the differences in factor ordering and significance of factor groups might well be just one more indication of a dialect difference. The resolution of that issue, however, is a topic for future research.

Table 5.7. Location: Comparison of Results for Southern Black ASL, Louisiana Black ASL, Northern Black ASL, and White ASL: Age by Lowering (% –cf)

Study	Tokens	Younger	Older	Total
southern Black ASL	877	36	23	29
Louisiana Black ASL	157	44	26	38
northern Black ASL (three sites)	555	50	32	47
White ASL (seven sites)	1,882	60	49	53

Note 1: Data for northern Black ASL and White ASL are from Lucas, Bayley, and Valli (2001). Data from White signers were collected in California, Kansas, Louisiana, Maryland, Massachusetts, Virginia, and Washington State. Data from northern African Americans were collected in California, Massachusetts, and Missouri. Results for Louisiana ASL are from Bayley and Lucas (in press a). The younger signers in Bayley and Lucas (in press a) and Lucas, Bayley, and Valli (2001) are age 54 and younger. Younger southern Black signers are 35 and younger. Older signers in all studies are 55+.

Although we cannot fully explain the differences between the two studies with respect to constraint ordering and the effects of the location and contact of the preceding and following signs, we can say that the variation in the location of signs such as KNOW in southern Black ASL is systematically constrained by both linguistic and social factors. In addition, we can provide clear answers to our first two research questions. First, southern Black signers produce far fewer noncitation variants of signs of the class examined here than the White signers who participated in the earlier study by Lucas, Bayley, and Valli (2001). Second, southern Black ASL seems to be changing, with younger signers much more likely to produce -cf forms than their elders.

To explore further the relationship between southern Black ASL and other ASL varieties, we compared the use of -cf forms of signs like KNOW with three other studies, as we did in the case of alternation between one-handed and two-handed signs. Table 5.7 and figure 5.4 show the results of the comparison, expressed in percentages of -cf forms by age group within each study. Note that all three African American groups choose the -cf variant at a lower rate than the White signers in the same age group and

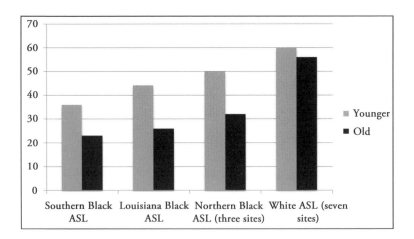

Figure 5.4. Location (lowering): Comparison of results for southern Black ASL, Louisiana Black ASL, northern Black ASL, and White ASL: Age by lowering (% –cf).

that, in every case, younger signers use more noncitation forms than older signers. The comparison across a range of Deaf communities suggests that the change that Frishberg (1975) identified is continuing.[13]

We turn now to the third phonological variable, the size of the signing space.

Size of the Signing Space

One of the anecdotal observations about Black ASL is that it uses a larger signing space (i.e., signs that exceed the rectangle that covers the area from the top of the head to the waist, from shoulder to shoulder, and a foot in front of the signer). When observers say about Black ASL, "Yeah, I see something different," it may be that a larger signing space is part of what they are seeing.

Other researchers have commented on the size of signing space. Lewis, Palmer, and Williams (1995) describe a signer comparing types of clothing and state that "The amount of body movements, mouth movements, and use of space are dramatically different in this individual's description of American and African clothing" (24), with the signer using a much larger space during the description of African clothing. Aramburo (1989) compares the signing of seven dyads. Dyad 3 consists of two Black Deaf signers, while dyads 6 and 7 consist of a Black Deaf signer and a White Deaf signer. Aramburo states that:

> the discourse in dyad 3 . . . differs from the discourse in dyads 6 and 7 with respect to facial expressions, body movement, and the size of the signing space used by the participants. The facial expressions are exaggerated in dyad 3, and both participants

---

13. Sociolinguists have long used the notion of apparent time to model language change (Bailey 2002). Research on a number of languages has shown that younger speakers (and signers) exhibit greater use of an incoming feature such as the lowering of signs like KNOW. Younger people also exhibit less frequent use of a receding feature (e.g., the two-handed versions of signs like DEER.

use their signing space to the fullest. In contrast, these two black deaf participants, X in dyad 6 and Y in dyad 7, use less exaggerated facial expressions, fewer body movements, and a smaller signing space when conversing with the white deaf participant than when conversing with each other. (117-18)

In addition, Tabak (2006), in a discussion of the children's signing at the Texas Blind, Deaf, and Orphan School in Austin, Texas, states that "the signs produced by the BDO students tend to be somewhat larger; that is, they use a larger signing space than their White contemporaries" (111). However, he offers no data as the basis for this observation.

Data for Size of Signing Space

As chapter 3 discusses, we created a corpus of cartoon retellings and free narratives that included both Black and White signers. As figure 5.5 illustrates, a grid was superimposed on each signer. The grid covers the area from the top of the signer's head to the signer's waist and from shoulder to shoulder, that is, the area in which conversational signing usually takes place.

Figure 5.5. Screen shot from ELAN showing signer with superimposed grid.

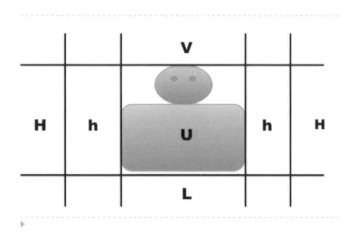

Figure 5.6. Labeled ELAN grid.

For coding, we used the EUDICO Linguistic Annotator (ELAN) annotation system developed at the Max Planck Institute and, as figure 5.6 shows, we distinguished the location of signs as follows:

U: unmarked, inside the usual signing space
V: extends above the top of the head
L: extends below the waist
h: extends beyond the shoulders
H: extends beyond raised elbows

For the VARBRUL analysis, we collapsed V, L, h, and H into one factor group, O, extending beyond the usual signing space, and this was the application value for the VARBRUL runs. Since grammatical category has proven to be significant for other phonological variables in sign languages, we coded for the grammatical category of signs as follows:

N: noun
A: adjective/adverb
P: plain verb (i.e., a verb that does not use space to indicate a grammatical relationship)

D: depiction/locative verb (i.e., a verb that may use space to indicate the relative location of the event or entity a signer is depicting)

I: indicating verb (i.e., a verb that uses space to indicate grammatical relationships)

F: function signs (e.g., pronouns, determiners, conjunctions, prepositions, interjections)

Obviously, verbs constitute a single grammatical category. Nevertheless, for the analysis of the size of the signing space, we could not simply put verbs into a single category. Because the depiction of an activity or an entity in space is integral to locative verbs, it stands to reason that these verbs might use a larger than usual signing space. Conversely, plain verbs do not usually exploit the signing space; thus, we would expect signers to produce them within the usual space.

We also coded for the relative intensity of the production of a sign: I = intense; N = not intense. By intensity, we mean noticeably more tension in the arms (the torso possibly leaning forward) and signing with furrowed eyebrows and a direct gaze at the cointerlocutor. Our hypothesis was that a larger signing space would be correlated with increased intensity.

Finally, we coded for the usual categories of age, gender, ethnicity, and genre.

Table 5.8. Size of the Signing Space: Distribution of Variants by Race

Variant	Black		White		Total	
	N	%	*N*	%	*N*	%
unmarked	671	58.5	724	65.8	1395	62.1
a foot away from the side of the body	322	28.1	268	24.4	590	26.3
more than a foot away from the side of the body	87	7.6	49	4.5	136	6.1
above the top of the head	43	3.7	36	3.3	79	3.5
below the waist	24	2.1	23	2.1	47	2.1

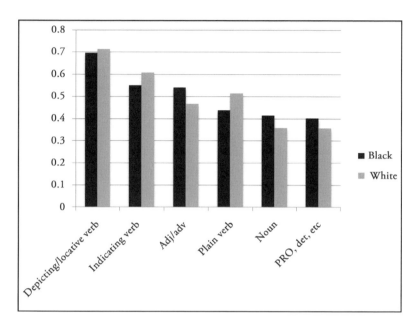

Figure 5.7. Size of the signing space: Grammatical category by race (VARBRUL weights).

Signing Space Results

Overall, both Black and White signers produced most of the signs coded within the usual signing space. The Black signers produced 58.5 percent of the signs coded within the usual space, while the White signers produced 65.8 percent. Table 5.8 summarizes the results for the five variants of the dependent variable for which we coded. Note that the Black signers produced a higher percentage of three of the four variants that exceeded the unmarked signing space. The only exception came in the very infrequent case in which signs were produced below the waist. In that case, the percentage of marked variants by Black and White signers was equal.

While the numbers and percentages of different variants shown in table 5.8 are suggestive, they do not yet answer the question of whether Black signers use a larger signing space than White signers. To address this question in greater depth, we employed multivariate analysis with VARBRUL.

Table 5.9. Size of the Signing Space: Black, White, and Combined Results (Application Value = Marked, i.e., Extends beyond the Usual Signing Space)

Factor Group	Factor	Black			White			Combined		
		Weight	%	N	Weight	%	N	Weight	%	N
grammatical category	depicting/locative verb	.698	67.9	237	.714	56.2	292	.703	61.4	529
	indicating verb	.551	50.0	40	.608	42.9	21	.597	47.5	61
	adj/adv	.542	43.4	173	.467	31.0	113	.511	38.5	286
	plain verb	.437	35.0	203	.515	37.4	206	.486	36.2	409
	noun	.414	31.1	254	.358	18.4	207	.391	25.4	461
	PRO, det. etc.	.401	29.2	240	.357	20.3	261	.371	24.6	501
intensity	more tension	.647	60.5	261	.779	66.4	214	.691	63.2	475
	normal	.455	35.9	886	.424	26.4	886	.446	31.2	1,792
age	35–	ns	40.6	652	.583	40.0	550	.539	40.3	1,202
	55+	ns	42.6	495	.417	28.5	550	.455	35.2	1,045
gender	male	.528	44.2	647	ns	34.2	600	.531	39.8	1,147
	female	.464	38.0	500	ns	34.2	500	.468	35.9	1,100

Factor Group	Factor	Black			White			Combined		
		Weight	%	N	Weight	%	N	Weight	%	N
race	Black		NA			NA		.539	41.5	1,147
	White		NA			NA		.460	33.5	1,100
genre	cartoon	.541	49.5	602	.424	34.0	600	ns	41.8	1,202
	free narrative	.455	32.7	545	.591	34.4	500	ns	33.5	1,045
total	input	.411	41.5	1147	.315	34.2	1100	.368	37.9	2,247

Notes: Black results: X^2/cell = 0.9793; log likelihood = −711.991; White results: X^2/cell = 1.4647, log likelihood = −599.745; combined results: X^2/cell = 1.2578, log likelihood = −1337.517.

"Not significant" is abbreviated as "ns."

Table 5.9 shows the results of three separate analyses: (1) Black signers only; (2) White signers only; (3) all signers combined. Figure 5.7 illustrates the results for grammatical category by Black and White signers. Recall that for these analyses all of the variants that extended beyond the unmarked signing space were combined. These marked variants were considered the application value, that is, the value of the dependent variable that counts as an application of the "rule" or process under investigation.

As table 5.9 shows, all of the factor groups for which we coded significantly affected the signers' use of a larger signing space. Thus, as expected, the grammatical category of the sign proved significant for both Black and White signers. Depicting and locative verbs were most likely to be extended beyond the unmarked space, followed by indicating verbs. Adjectives and adverbs slightly favored the use of a marked variant by Black signers (.542) and slightly disfavored the use of a marked variant by White signers (.467). Plain verbs, nouns, pronouns, and function signs disfavored the use of a marked variant by both groups. Moreover, the constraint ranking was identical for Black and White signers.

Like grammatical category, the intensity factor group showed similar results for both Black and White signers. In fact, intensity proved to be the first-order constraint in all of the analyses. As hypothesized, signs produced with indications of greater intensity were more likely to extend beyond the usual signing space (.691 in the combined analysis).

Although the results for grammatical category and intensity show little difference between Black and White signers (at least in constraint ordering), the results for the social factors present a different picture. Only the results for gender, which show that women are less likely to use a larger signing space than men, are the same for the two groups. The results for age (see figure 5.8) are particularly interesting. Note that, for Black signers, age does not reach statistical significance. Although the older signers produced a slightly higher percentage of marked variants, the difference between the older and the younger groups was not greater than could be attributed to chance (42.6% vs. 40.6%). However, for the White signers, the difference was highly significant. Only 28.5 percent of the signs produced by older White signers extended beyond the usual signing space, with a factor weight

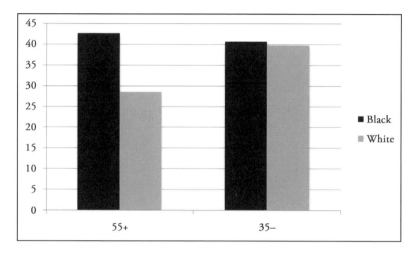

Figure 5.8. Size of the signing space: Age by race (percentage of signs beyond the usual signing space).

of .417. In contrast, 40 percent of the signs produced by the younger White signers extended beyond the normal signing space, with a factor weight of .583. That is, with respect to this variable, younger White signers appear to be signing more like Black signers than like the older White signers.

The final difference between the two groups concerns the effects of genre. As table 5.9 shows, the cartoon narratives favored the use of a marked variant by Black signers (.541), while the free narratives favored the use of a marked variant by White signers (.591). The reasons for this difference are unclear. We suggest that further work is needed to determine whether the difference is consistent across other groups or whether it represents an epiphenomenon.

BLACK ASL AS A CONSERVATIVE DIALECT

The results of our analyses of the three phonological variables-alternation between one-handed and two-handed signs, the variable lowering of signs like KNOW, and the size of the signing space-suggest that southern Black ASL is a generally conservative dialect that adheres more closely to

Table 5.10. Overall Likelihood (Input) of Use of One-Handed Variant, Lowered (–cf) Variant, and Size of Signing Space

Study	One-Hand vs. Two-Hand		Location (Lowering)		Use of Larger Signing Space	
	Tokens	Input	Tokens	Input	Tokens	Input
southern Black ASL	818	.336	877	.260	1147	.411
Louisiana Black ASL	258	.378	157	.377	no data	
northern Black ASL	855	.443	555	.468	no data	
White ASL	1,115	.505	1,882	.558	1,100	.315

Notes: See Table 5.7 for data source information.

prescriptive norms than does White ASL. This suggestion is clearly confirmed by the data presented in table 5.10, which shows the input values, or corrected means, for handedness and location in four different populations: the signers in this study; the Louisiana African Americans; the northern African Americans; and the White signers from Lucas, Bayley, and Valli (2001). In every case, African Americans are less likely to use the one-handed or the lowered variant. Table 5.10 also includes the input values for the size of the signing space in the current study. In the case of the size of the signing space (in contrast to the other two variables), a higher input value indicates a more traditional variant (i.e., more frequent use of signs that extend beyond the central signing space).

Finally, Table 5.11 shows percentages of use of one-handed signs, lowered signs, and signs produced within the unmarked signing space divided by age and race. The data for one-handed signs produced by White signers are from Lucas et al. 2007, while the data for lowering are from Lucas, Bayley, and Valli (2001). The data from the size of the signing space are from the current study. Note that, except for the case of the size of the signing space, where younger White signers seem to be converging with

Table 5.11. Use of One-Handed Variant, Lowered (−cf) Variant, and Size of the Signing Space by Age and Race

	Younger		Older	
Variable	Southern Black	White	Southern Black	White
one-hand (%)	40	57	35	37
location (% −cf, lowered)	36	61	23	50
signing space (% in the unmarked space)	59	60	58	71

Notes: See Table 5.7 for data source information.

younger Black signers, the Black signers use a higher percentage of the more traditional form.

These results, shown in three variables that differ in important respects, raise a question: Why should African American Deaf signers be more likely than White signers to use more traditional forms? At present, we do not have sufficient evidence to provide a definitive answer. We are able, however, to point to evidence that suggests a possible explanation. Recall our discussion of the rise of oralism in chapter 2. As Baynton (1996) has noted, in what we regard as a stunning misapplication of Darwinian evolutionary theory, spoken languages have historically been regarded as being more highly evolved than sign languages. In addition, according to the racial notions prevalent in the late nineteenth and early twentieth centuries, Black people were regarded as being less highly evolved than White people. As a consequence, oralism was not as rigorously enforced in schools for African American deaf children as it was in the White deaf schools. A paradoxical effect of racism and misunderstanding of a scientific theory caused many Black deaf children to receive an education that was more comprehensible than the education their White deaf counterparts received. The facilities in the Black deaf schools were inferior, to be sure, but the fact that ASL was used in the formal atmosphere of the classroom in at least some schools for

Black deaf children at least partially explains the results that we have seen in this chapter. Black ASL is more conservative and adheres more closely to prescriptive norms than White ASL because, during the era of segregation, a substantial number of Black deaf children attended schools that employed adult signing role models and used ASL as a medium of education.

6

Variation in Syntax and Discourse

In examining Black ASL syntax and discourse, we focus on the use of repetition, constructed action, and constructed dialogue. By "the use of repetition," we mean the complete repetition of a single sign or a phrase by one signer within one turn. While we review some of the earlier work on the use of repetition in ASL and other sign languages, there is no specific claim in the literature that Black signers use repetition more than do other signers. The decision to focus on this feature came strictly from reviewing videotaped interviews conducted with Black signers as we were planning and seeking funding for the project. We observed a lot of repetition, and this seemed to be an interesting feature to explore. Indeed, two older Arkansas signers on our tapes specifically mention repetition as a difference between Black and White signing. As for constructed action and constructed dialogue, there are some specific claims that Black signers use both constructions more than White signers do, and we therefore wanted to collect empirical data to explore the validity of those claims.

The use of repetition in ASL and other sign languages has been discussed by other researchers, mainly in the context of Chomskyan analyses of *wh*-movement. Petronio and Lillo-Martin (1997) mention "a very commonly found type of ASL WH-question, in which a WH-element is found both sentence initially and sentence finally." The examples they provide are "WHO LIKE NANCY WHO?" (where WHO is the subject) and "WHAT NANCY BUY WHAT?" (where WHAT is the object) (26) They also describe non-*wh*

We gratefully acknowledge Emily Talbot and Anika Stephen's contributions to this chapter.

doubles, "which can occur with elements such as modals, quantifiers, and verbs" and are "used for focus or emphasis in ASL" (29-30). Neidle et al. (2000) state that "Questions containing more than one WH-phrase corresponding to a single questioned argument are quite common in ASL" (114) and describe both final tags with *wh*-phrases and initial WH-topics. However, as far as we know, no one has studied the kind of repetition that we have found in our data: the immediate repetition (two or more times) of elements ranging from nouns, adjectives, adverbs, and function words (including pronouns) to verb phrases, full sentences, and token responses. Interestingly, of the 172 examples that we analyzed, only two involve the repetition of a *wh*-word. Petronio and Lillo-Martin's (1997) mention of "focus and emphasis" may apply here, and what we may be looking at, therefore, is a discourse phenomenon with syntactic consequences.

REPETITION

Our goal was to compare the amount of repetition used by Black signers and White signers, and we wanted to avoid being influenced by anecdotal impressions that one group uses more repetition than another. To this end, from a set of 95 clips, we randomly selected 12 ten-minute clips of conversations from our Black ASL data (6 from the "over 55" group and 6 from the "under 35" group) and did the same from the data used in Lucas, Bayley, and Valli (2001) for the White signers, for an initial total of 24 clips. We used the same clips for our analysis of voiceless mouthing (chapter 7), and, as a result of coding for mouthing, an additional "over 55" Black female was added and also an "over 55" White male, the latter because of his total lack of mouthing, in sharp contrast to his wife, sitting next to him, who mouthed continuously. This resulted in 26 clips analyzed for the use of repetition. Since these clips were randomly selected, we did not control for geographic region.

We coded each clip for the total number of repetition events. That is, an utterance in which the same sign phrase was repeated at least twice was counted as *one* event, not as two or three. For example, when one male signer in the "over 55" group signed BETTER, BETTER, BETTER in response to a question, we counted this as one instance of repetition. We also coded what was being repeated in terms of form and function as follows:

> noun: #DAY STUDENT, #DAY STUDENT? [question directed at another signer]
> adjective/adverb: 2-DAY-AGO . . . 2-DAY-AGO, 2-DAY-AGO[response]
> verb/predicate: SAME, LEAVE, LEAVE, LEAVE, LEAVE.
> *wh*-sign: KILL, WHY, WHY?
> function word (including pronouns): PRO.I, PRO.I, THAT
> verb phrase/full sentence: PRO.2 BRAVE, PRO.2 BRAVE.
> token response: RIGHT, RIGHT, RIGHT, RIGHT [response]

The category verb/predicate is justified since many signs that might ordinarily be considered adjectives (e.g., SICK) or nouns (e.g., HOME) can function as predicates in ASL. As for verb phrase/full sentence, we were most likely to find verb phrases repeated. For events in this category, we coded only if the phrase or sentence was immediately and fully repeated. We counted responses and instances of back-channeling such as RIGHT and TRUE as token responses. We did not code for events in which the repetition was clearly morphological in nature (e.g., LEARN, LEARN, LEARN) where the signer's meaning was clearly "repeatedly learn" as opposed to a simple repetition of the lexical sign. We also kept in mind signs in which repetition is a part of the structure. For example, CHURCH is usually signed with two contacts of the dominant hand on the base hand. This was not counted as an instance of repetition, of course. However, one signer signed this sign with six total contacts, clearly three instances of the sign, so we counted this as an example of repetition.

Table 6.1 shows the breakdown of examples by grammatical form/function and by individual signer. Table 6.2 summarizes the data by race, age, and gender.

Tables 6.1 and 6.2 show that verb/predicate and verb phrase/full sentence are the categories in which repetition is most likely to occur, followed by nouns. Some adjectives and adverbs are also subject to repetition, as opposed to *wh*-signs and function words such as pronouns. The question arises as to

Table 6.1. Repetition by Grammatical Function

Signer	State	Eth.	Age	Sex	Noun	Adj/ Adv	Verb/ Pred	WH	Function Sign (incl. PRO)	Verb Phrase/Full Sentence	Token Response	Total
1	AL	B	o	f	2	1	4	0	0	1	4	12
2	AL	B	o	f	0	0	2	2	1	0	1	6
3	AR	B	o	m	0	0	7	0	1	0	0	8
4	LA	B	o	m	3	0	10	0	1	7	0	21
5	NC	B	o	f	1	0	3	0	1	13	2	20
6	TX	B	o	m	4	3	2	0	0	9	0	18
7	VA	B	o	m	3	1	1	0	0	3	1	9
8	AL	B	y	f	1	0	1	0	0	2	6	10
9	AR	B	y	f	3	0	0	0	0	2	0	5
10	LA	B	y	m	4	0	0	0	0	1	0	5
11	NC	B	y	m	3	1	0	0	0	6	1	11
12	TX	B	y	f	0	1	0	0	0	4	0	5
13	VA	B	y	f	0	0	0	0	0	4	2	6
Subtotal Black					24	7	30	2	4	52	17	136
14	KS	W	o	f	0	0	1	0	0	0	0	1

15	MD	W	o	f	1	1	0	0	0	0	0	2
16	MD	W	o	m	2	1	5		0	7	3	18
17	MD	W	o	f	1	0	0	0	0	1	0	2
18	VA	W	o	m	0	0	0	0	0	0	0	0
19	VA	W	o	m	0	0	1	0	0	0	0	1
20	WA	W	o	f	0	0	0	0	0	0	0	0
21	MA	W	y	f	1	0	1	0	1	0	0	3
22	MD	W	y	m	1	1	0	0	0	0	0	2
23	LA	W	y	f	0	1	1	0	0	5	0	7
24	LA	W	y	m	0	0	0	0	0	2		2
25	VA	W	y	m	1	0	0	0	0	0	0	1
26	WA	W	y	m	0	0	1	0	0	2	0	4
Subtotal White					7	4	10	0	1	17	3	43
Total					31	11	40	2	5	63	20	172

Note: AL = Alabama; AR = Arkansas; KS = Kansas; LA = Louisiana; MD = Maryland; MA = Massachusetts; NC = North Carolina; TX = Texas; VA = Virginia; WA = Washington State.

Table 6.2. Repetition by Grammatical Function by Race, Gender, and Age

Group	Noun	Adj/Adv	Verb/Pred	WH	Function Sign (incl. PRO)	Verb Phrase/ Full Sentence	Token Response	Total
Black male, older	10	4	20	0	2	14	1	51
Black female, older	3	1	9	2	2	13	7	37
Black male, younger	7	1	0	0	0	7	1	16
Black female, younger	4	1	1	0	0	12	8	26
White male, older	2	1	6	0	0	7	3	19*
White female, older	2	1	1	0	0	1	0	5
White male, younger	2	1	1	0	0	4	0	8
White female, younger	1	1	2	0	1	5	0	10
Total	31	11	40	2	5	63	20	172

* Eighteen were from one signer.

Table 6.3. Number of Questions (vs. Declaratives) by Grammatical Function

Grammatical function	Noun	Adj/Adv	Verb/Pred	WH	Function Word (incl. PRO)	VP/Full S	Token Response	Total
Black male, older	1/10	0/4	1/20	0	1/2	4/14	0/1	7/51
Black female, older	1/3	0/1	0/9	1/2	0/2	1/13	0/7	3/37
Black male, younger	0/6	0/1	0	0	0	3/8	0/1	3/16
Black female, younger	0/4	0/1	0/1	0	0	1/12	0/8	1/26
White male, older	0/2	0/1	0/6	0	0	2/7	0/3	2/19*
White female, older	1/2	0/1	0/1	0	0	0/1	0	1/5
White male, younger	0/2	0/1	0/1	0	0	2/4	0	2/8
White female, younger	0/1	0/1	0/2	0	1/1	4/5	v	5/10
Total	3/31	0/11	1/40	1/2	2/5	17/63	0/20	24/172

whether these verb phrases and full sentences are declarative or interrogative. That is, the repetition could be a function of the fact that the signer is asking a question. Table 6.3 shows the breakdown of items in all grammatical categories by declarative and interrogative and by race, age, and gender.

As table 6.3 shows, 24 of the 172 repetitions were questions, and most of these were full verb phrases or full sentences: 14 for Black signers, 10 for White signers. We found only one example of the repetition of a *wh*-sign as a question. We found 11 repetitions of adjectives or adverbs and 40 of verbs/predicates. Only one of those 51 occurred in a question. Repetition seems to have a function of emphasis and does not appear to be used for clarification.

As table 6.4 shows, the 47 declaratives are rarely responses to questions by other signers. Most of the time, the repetition of a verb phrase or a full sentence appears to emphasize a point. Finally, although the use of repetition in response to a question from another signer is rare, the three examples that we do have are all from Black signers.

Here we see a striking difference between Black signers and White signers in the use of repetition, with Black signers, both old and young, showing three times the number of repetitions as those found among the White signers. This is evident also within the specific age categories. It is particularly striking when we consider that 18 of the 19 examples from older White signers were produced by one signer. Without those 18 instances, the ratio becomes 57 instances from the Black signers compared to 1 from the White signers.

It would seem, then, that repetition is a feature that distinguishes Black signers from White signers. Indeed, the differences between Black and White signers are quite striking. We also see an interesting change in the Black population, with more repetition among the older signers than among the younger ones. What seems to be occurring here, then, is much like what is occurring with other variables. Integration has resulted in a partial convergence of Black and White ASL varieties, whether in the number of citation forms in the case of lowering or two-handed signs or in characteristics that have nothing to do with the citation/noncitation distinction such as repetition, which seems to have a pragmatic function. The idea that repetition serves a pragmatic function is supported by the fact repetitions in all grammatical categories are predominantly declarative statements rather than questions.

Table 6.4. Repetitions in Declarative Sentences by Race, Gender, and Age

Group	Repetition Is a Response to a Question	Repetition Is Not a Response to a Question	Total
Black male, older	2	8	10
Black female, older	0	12	12
Black male, younger	1	4	5
Black female, younger	0	11	11
White male, older	0	5	5
White female, older	0	1	1
White male, younger	0	2	2
White female, younger	0	1	1
Total	3	44	47

Table 6.5 summarizes the use of repetition by race, age, and gender.

Table 6.5. Repetition by Race, Gender, and Age

Age and Gender	Black	White	Total
Older, male (8)	51	19*	70
Older, female (6)	37	5	42
Younger, male (6)	16	8	24
Younger, female (6)	26	10	36
Total: 26	130	42	172

Note: *18 instances from one signer

Constructed Action and Constructed Dialogue

A number of studies have addressed what Tannen (1989) refers to as constructed action and constructed dialogue, which are commonly referred to as "taking the role." As Metzger (1995) explains, it is the way that signers "use their body, head and eye gaze to report the actions, thoughts, words and expressions of characters within a discourse" (256) (see also Roy 1989). Dudis (2004) has also examined this phenomenon in detail in his exploration of real-space blends and of body partitioning, whereby "different parts of [a] signer's body [are] projected as separate visible real-space elements into their respective blends" (225). We wanted to examine the use of constructed action and constructed dialogue in this project because previous research indicates that Black signers may utilize them more than White signers. Metzger and Mather (2004) analyzed nineteen narratives that occurred during the course of natural conversations and compared the use of constructed action and constructed dialogue by five Black signers and three White signers. They found sixty-eight instances of constructed action (CA), twenty-five of constructed dialogue (CD), and fifty-four of constructed action and constructed dialogue together (CA/CD). Table 6.6 summarizes their results.

We see from table 6.6 that the Black male signers used markedly more CA and CA/CD but did not use CD by itself. Metzger and Mather (2004) also note that both the Black males and the Black females used CA/CD

Table 6.6. Use of Constructed Action (CA) and Constructed Dialogue (CD) by White and Black Signers

Signers	CA	CD	CA/CD	Total
White men	13	2	11	26
Black men	33	0	27	60
White women	16	15	13	44
Black women	6	4	9	19

Source: Metzger and Mather (2004).

together, with complete eye-gaze detachment, while the White signers used CA before CD was introduced. As far as we know, Metzger and Mather's study is the only research that compares CA and CD use in Black and White signers.

Data and Methods: Constructed Action and Constructed Dialogue

In order to compare the use of CA and CD by Black and White signers, we analyzed two kinds of data: retellings of the plots of wordless cartoons and narratives that occurred naturally in videotaped conversations. Table 6.7 summarizes the data for the CA/CD analysis.

Using the ELAN (Eudico Linguistic Annotator), we coded both the cartoon narratives and the free narratives according to seven different possible events as follows:

1. constructed action (CA): a full instance of constructed action with a signer as X (Dudis 2004) and parts of the body recruited as part of the X's character's body movement

    Example: the signer takes the role of someone driving a car

2. constructed dialogue (CD): a full instance of constructed dialogue with a signer as X producing signs as a dialogue from X

    Example: Signing as his mother, the signer signs PRO.I WANT PRO.2 EXPE-RIENCE SURROUNDING BUT WHEN HOME NOT BRING THAT HOME ("I want you to experience the surroundings but don't bring that home.")

Table 6.7. Narrative Types Used in the Analysis of Constructed Action and Constructed Dialogue

Signers	Cartoon Narratives	Conversation Narratives
Black, older	6	4
Black, younger	6	7
White, older	7	4
White, younger	5	6
Total	24	21

Table 6.8. Summary of Constructed Action and Constructed Dialogue Events

Signers	CA	CD	CABP	CDBP	CACD	CANA	Total
Black male, older	60	11	35	3	0	3	112
Black female, older	18	57	38	0	1	8	122
Black male, middle aged	12	9	0	0	0	0	21
Black male, younger	52	50	25	1	2	10	140
Black female, younger	39	12	36	2	3	19	111
White male, older	77	39	53	2	1	0	172
White female, older	66	20	42	3	0	4	135
White male, middle aged	5	9	1	0	1	0	16
White female, middle aged	8	4	1	0	0	0	13
White male, younger	20	6	22	0	1	10	59
White female, younger	39	27	42	0	1	11	120
Total	396	244	295	11	9	65	1,021

Notes: The clips were selected randomly. No middle-aged Black females were selected. See pages 118–121 for an explanation of abbreviations of events.

3. constructed action/body partitioning (CABP): a simultaneous instance of constructed action with a signer as X and a part of the body partitioned to depict an event

    Example: The signer turns her head away to show that she is trying to avoid water hitting her in the face while one hand simultaneously uses a 3 handshape to represent a jet ski that is still moving.

4. constructed dialogue/body partitioning (CDBP): a simultaneous instance of constructed dialogue with a signer as X producing signs on one hand and using the other hand to depict an event

    Example: One of the signer's hands uses a 3 handshape to represent a stopped vehicle while the other signs COME-ON.

5. constructed action/constructed dialogue (CACD): a simultaneous instance of constructed action and external or internal constructed dialogue

    Example: In the role of a dog holding a light bulb, the signer signs SICK #DO DO? ("What a pain. What am I going to do?")

6. constructed action/narrative (CANA): an instance of constructed action with a signer as X and signs produced as a plain narrative

    Example: In the role of a rabbit, the signer signs REVENGE IX-LF (pointing left) and then signs DOG as part of the narrative.

7. constructed dialogue/narrative (CDNA): an instance of constructed dialogue with a signer as X and signs produced as plain narrative

    Example: This is extremely rare, and we found no examples.

With the ELAN software, we were able to clearly compare the overall use of CA and CD by Black signers and White signers and also the use of specific kinds of CA and CD. We looked at a total of 1,021 examples. Table 6.8 shows how many examples of each type we analyzed.

As tables 6.9 and 6.10 show, the cartoon narratives varied considerably in length, ranging from 58.40 to 73.33 seconds, while the narratives that occurred in free conversation varied even more in the extent of elaboration, ranging from 46.67 to 139.50 seconds.

Table 6.9. Time (in Seconds): Cartoon Narratives

Seconds	Average	Minimum	Maximum	
Black	older	73.33	67.00	83.00
	younger	84.33	58.00	158.00
White	older	99.71	63.00	178.00
	younger	58.40	47.00	67.00

In tables 6.11 and 6.12, we see the average number of units for narrative, constructed action, and constructed dialogue by age and race. There are no striking differences in the average number of various unit types produced by White signers and Black signers in the cartoon narratives. This may be the effect of the focused situation of elicitation. However, in the free narratives, older signers, both Black and White, use simple narrative (NA) more than do the younger signers. However, as the time differences in table 6.10 suggest, the difference in the use of narrative units by age may simply reflect the greater length of the older signers' narratives. Older White signers supply more units of constructed action than older Black signers, while the narratives of older Black signers have more instances of constructed dialogue (CD) than the narratives of the White signers. This result contrasts with the results reported by Metzger and Mather (2004), who found that Black males used more CA and CACD than White signers but never used CD by itself.

We need to treat the results in tables 6.11 and 6.12, however, with considerable caution because all of the narratives, but especially the free

Table 6.10. Time (in Seconds): Free Narratives

Seconds	Average	Minimum	Maximum	
Black	older	139.50	23.00	194.00
	younger	121.29	40.00	295.00
White	older	115.00	32.00	181.00
	younger	46.67	25.00	77.00

Table 6.11. Average Number of Narrative Units, Constructed Action Units, and Constructed Dialogue Units for Cartoon Narratives by Race and Age

	Black		White	
	Older	Younger	Older	Younger
narrative	12.67	16.17	15.71	11.80
constructed action	9.17	11.67	13.43	9.80
constructed dialogue	1.67	2.50	3.71	3.80
constructed action/ narrative	0	4.50	.57	4.20
constructed action, body positioning	10.33	7.00	.71	9.20
constructed action/ constructed dialogue	0	.67	0	.40

Table 6.12. Average Number of Narrative Units, Constructed Action, and Constructed Dialogue Units for Free Narratives by Race and Age

	Black		White	
	Older	Younger	Older	Younger
narrative	20.25	10.00	18.75	9.67
constructed action	5.75	4.71	12.25	3.83
constructed dialogue	14.50	8.00	8.25	4.50
constructed action/ narrative	2.75	.29	0	0
constructed action, body positioning	2.75	2.71	7.75	3.33
constructed action/ constructed dialogue	.25	.14	.25	.17

narratives, show a great deal of individual variation. For example, among the free narratives produced by the older Black signers, the number of constructed action units varies from a low of only 1 to a high of 15. The range among the units of constructed dialogue is even greater (6 to 41). We have a similarly large range among the White signers. One older White signer, for example, supplied no instances of constructed action in her free narrative; the free narrative of another signer contained 26 constructed action units.

Figures 6.1 and 6.2, which take the difference in narrative length into account, provide another comparison of the use of constructed action and constructed dialogue by age and race. Figure 6.1 shows the average proportion of time for narrative units and units of constructed action and constructed dialogue. Figure 6.2 provides the same information for the narratives embedded in free conversation. In both cases, we have combined the units of CA/body positioning and narrative/CA under the more general category of CA and CD/body positioning and narrative/CD under the more general category of CD.

As figure 6.1 shows, constructed action occupied a greater portion of the narratives produced by Black signers, both young and old, than by

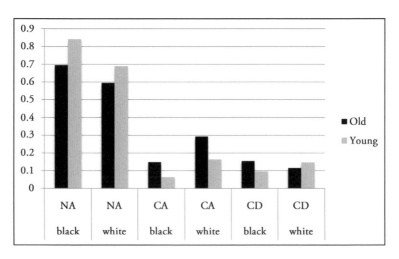

Notes: CA includes CA/BP and NACA, CD includes CDBP and NACD.

Figure 6.1. Average proportion of time for each unit in the cartoon narratives.

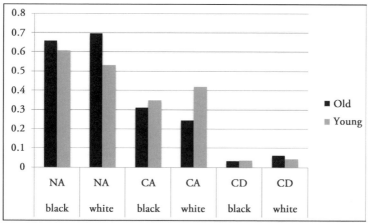

Notes: CA includes CA/BP and NACA, CD includes CDBP and NACD

Figure 6.2. Average proportion of time for each unit in the free narratives.

White signers. Constructed dialogue also occupied a greater portion of the cartoon narratives produced by older Black signers.

Constructed dialogue is one of the features in the mosaic that we discussed in chapter 1. Our data suggest that it is used more by Black signers than by White signers, both young and old, although there is a great deal of individual variation. Clearly these possible differences merit further investigation.

To sum up, then, we have clear evidence that Black signers, especially older ones, use more repetition than White signers. With constructed action and constructed dialogue, our conclusions must be much more tentative given the extent of individual variation.

7

The Effects of Language Contact

In this chapter we look at the effects of the contact between Black ASL and spoken English to see whether they help make Black ASL a distinct variety. We look specifically at the use of mouthing of English words and the incorporation of features from African American English. Our interest in voiceless mouthing was sparked during data collection when we noticed that a number of signers, both old and young, and particularly those from Texas and Alabama, were not mouthing at all when they signed. We started to wonder whether this might be one of the features that we were looking for. The only reference that we have been able to find is in Tabak (2006), who remarks, "[M]any graduates of TSD [Texas School for the Deaf, the school for White students] tend to voicelessly pronounce certain important words . . . This is much less common among BDO [the Texas Blind, Deaf, and Orphan School in Austin, Texas] graduates, who, free from any perceived relations between signs and the spoken word, use their facial expressions in ways that depend not at all on lip reading" (111). This, however, seems to be Tabak's personal observation and not a conclusion based on research. As for the incorporation of AAE features, Black Deaf signers of course have extended contact with speakers of AAE and also with the aspects of popular culture in which AAE features occur. It stands to reason that some of these features would be incorporated into Black ASL, and we wanted to identify them.

RESEARCH ON MOUTHING

Many studies have focused on mouthing as used by White signers. A major work is the 2001 volume coedited by Boyes Braem and Sutton-Spence, *The Hands Are the Head of the Mouth,* which presents accounts of mouthing in a number of sign languages, including Norwegian Sign Language (NSL, Vogt-Svendsen), Finnish Sign Language (FinSL, Rainò), Swedish Sign Language (Bergman and Wallin), British Sign Language (BSL, Sutton-Spence and Day 2001; Woll 2001), Swiss German Sign Language (DSGS, Boyes Braem), German Sign Language (DGS, Ebbinghaus and Hessmann; Hohenberger and Happ; Keller), Italian Sign Language (LIS, Ajello, Mazzoni, and Nicolai), Indo-Pakistani Sign Language (IPSL, Zeshan), and Sign Language of the Netherlands (SLN, Schermer). The first major issue addressed by all of the researchers concerns the distinction between *mouthing* (i.e., the events that are derived from the spoken language) and *mouth gestures* (i.e., those events that are part of the sign language and have no relation to the spoken language). In ASL, the former can be illustrated with the mouth configuration "f-sh," which might accompany FINISH. This mouthing might be more complete, such that a signer might silently mouth a whole English word. A good example of a mouth gesture, on the other hand, would be the voiceless mouth configuration "pah" that accompanies the sign glossed as FINALLY or AT LAST. This configuration is indigenous to the sign language and has no relation to any English word. Our focus, of course, is on the mouthing of English words.

The researchers who contributed to Boyes Braem and Sutton-Spence (2001) also explored a second major issue: the extent of the mouthing (i.e., whether the spoken-language word is fully or just partially mouthed). Hohenberger and Happ (2001) distinguish between "full" and "restricted" mouthings (153), while Vogt-Svendsen refers to words being "shortened" (2001, 14). For Italian Sign Language, Ajello, Mazzoni, and Nicolai (2001) refer to "a tendency to chop the word at the tonic vowel" (233). This distinction between full and partial mouthing was first studied by Davis (1989) in his study of English-to-ASL interpretation. His data suggested:

> a range of mouthing. . . . At one extreme is what can be aptly described as a unique kind of code-mixing, the use of ASL simultaneously with the mouthing of English words. . . . At the other extreme is ASL mouthing, which does not encode

English. . . . Between these two extremes of full English mouthing and ASL mouthing, there is reduced English mouthing,
which for now is best described as a kind of lexical borrowing.
(95–96)

Lucas and Valli (1992) also address the issue of mouthing in their study of
contact signing. While the other researchers mentioned have studied the
dimensions of the mouthing—full or restricted, reduced, chopped—Lucas
and Valli also looked at the duration of the mouthing (i.e., whether it was
continuous or intermittent) and suggested that the continuous mouthing
that they observed was a key feature of contact signing.

The third major issue concerns the relationship between mouthing
and the grammatical class or function of the English item that a signer is
mouthing. As Boyes Braem and Sutton-Spence (2001) point out,
"Repeatedly, contributors describe more mouthings with nouns and
uninflected forms of verbs, while mouth gestures are seen more with
verbs" (4). More recently, Nadolske and Rosenstock (2007) find that
nouns and adjectives reflected high levels of mouthing, followed by
adverbs and plain verbs. Directional verbs, pronouns, and classifiers
(depicting verbs) had noticeably lower levels, while classifiers had the
least.

Nadolske and Rosenstock also raise a fourth issue, that of attitudes
toward mouthing: "Within the ASL research and Deaf communities, the
presence of mouthings has been considered solely a contact phenomenon
and discounted as a part of 'real' ASL, where 'real' ASL refers to natural
conversations where only Deaf participants are present" (2–3). They go on
to point out that the rejection of mouthing as a component of a natural
sign language is by no means universal: "Many of the world's sign language
communities accept mouthings as an integral part of their sign language"
(3), as Boyes Braem and Sutton-Spence (2001) clearly show. For Italian
Sign Language (LIS), Ajello, Mazzoni, and Nicolai (2001) point out the
strong role of the oral language, which "was particularly promoted in the
schooling and lives of deaf people" (2001, 235), often to the exclusion of
sign languages. Given the history of deaf education with its focus on

oralism, the continued presence of mouthing in indigenous sign languages is not at all surprising.

Mouthing in sign languages, then, has been fairly extensively examined. We now turn to our data, starting with a description of how we collected the information.

How We Looked at Mouthing and Why

Given the anecdotes and general claims that Black signers use mouthing less than White signers do, we wanted to base our analysis on a sample that was as objective as possible. We used the same dataset that we used for our analysis of repetition (chapter 6): 26 ten-minute clips selected randomly from a set of 95 clips: 7 for older Black signers, 6 for younger Black signers, 7 for older White signers, and 6 for younger White signers. We coded by grammatical class and function as follows (the sign glosses for the mouthed words are shown):

nouns: for example, ENGLISH

adjectives and adverbs: HAPPY, MORE

verbs and predicates: WORK, SICK

wh-words: WHY

function words, including pronouns: YOU

phrases (which sometimes included whole sentences): THAT OLD-FASHIONED SIGN ("That's an old-fashioned sign.")

reactive tokens (i.e., when a signer signs RIGHT, TRUE, or UNDERSTAND as a function of back-channeling or responding without further elaboration): Since we had coded reactive tokens for repetition, we also expected them to be mouthed but found no examples occurring alone.

Since the clips were randomly selected, we did not code for geographical region.

Table 7.1. Mouthing by Grammatical Class/Function, Race, Age, and Gender

Signer	Noun	Adj/adv	Verb/Predicate	WH	Function Word	Phrase	Token Response	Total
OBM	22	8	13	3	0	0	0	46
OBF	11	6	25	3	4	0	0	49
YBM	24	11	15	1	0	13	0	64
YBF	6	9	3	1	4	16	0	39
Subtotal	63	34	56	8	8	29	0	198
OWM	3	0	2	0	1	0	0	6
OWF	*	*	*	*	*	*	*	*
YWM	6	0	1	0	2	8	0	17
YWF	*	*	*	*	*	*	*	*
Subtotal	9	0	3	0	3	8	0	23
Total	72	34	59	8	11	37	0	221

Notes: OBM = old, Black, male; OBF = old, Black, female; OWM = old, White, male, OWF = old, White, female, YBM = young, Black, male, YBF = young, Black, female, YWM = young, White, male, YWF = young, White, female.

Table 7.2. Continuous Mouthing by Age, Race, and Gender

Signers	Mouthed Continuously
young Black females	3 out of 4
young White females	1 out of 2
young White males	3 out of 4
older White females	3 out of 3
older White males	1 out of 4
Total	11 out of 26 total signers

What We Found

Table 7.1 summarizes our findings by grammatical class/function, race, age, and gender.

We see in table 7.1 that, as other researchers have found, nouns were the most frequently mouthed, followed by plain verbs and predicates, phrases, and finally adjectives and adverbs. Some function words were mouthed, as well as a small number of wh-words. Other researchers have not commented on the mouthing of phrases or whole sentences, but we observed a number of them, mostly among the young Black signers. What is important here is that the countable instances of mouthing are all examples of very "light" intermittent mouthing (i.e., perhaps just part of an initial consonant or a consonant and vowel combination). Examples include just the initial p and the initial a in the phrase "pay attention," the initial vowel in "agree," and the initial consonant and vowel in "wife." That is to say, the mouthing is not even close to the full words/phrases "pay attention," "agree," or "wife." It is very close to the restricted mouthing mentioned by Hohenberger and Happ (2001) for DGS, the Norwegian Sign Language reductions of Vogt-Svendsen (2001), and the Italian Sign Language "chopping" mentioned by Ajello, Mazzoni, and Nicolai (2001). It is the reduced mouthing, sometimes drastically reduced, that Davis (1989) also mentions. Moreover, at first glance it appears that the Black signers mouthed more than did the White signers, 198 instances as opposed to 23. However, table 7.1 represents the *countable* instances of individual mouthings within discourses where no other mouthing occurred. This does not represent the whole picture of what we found. In table 7.1, older White females and young White females are both marked with an asterisk. What we see with the asterisked groups is continuous voiceless mouthing, for which it is simply impossible to count individual instances. Table 7.2 shows the breakdown by age, race, and gender for this continuous mouthing.

In some cases, this continuous mouthing looks like the contact signing that Lucas and Valli (1992) have described. In other cases, what is happening on the hands has the structure of ASL syntax. It is accompanied by this continuous light mouthing, which consistently stops when the signer produces a depicting verb (classifier). For example, a young Black woman in Alabama lightly mouthed FIRST MOVE and then produced an ASL mouth gesture with the sign AWKWARD. An older White woman in Maryland was continuously mouthing while describing a school building but stopped while she produced a depicting verb for the wheelchair ramp. With this sign, she produced the appropriate mouth gesture. Other researchers have noticed this phenomenon as well.

It is also very striking to see that the older Black males, the older Black females, and the younger Black males as groups had only intermittent individual instances of mouthing. They showed no continuous mouthing at all. There seems to be, therefore, an age effect among the Black signers and a gender effect between the younger Black women and the younger Black males. We have been able to sample only a relatively small portion of the large corpus collected for this project, and, based on that sample, we cannot say definitively that Black signers mouth less than White signers do. The results of our study of this sample suggest, however, that older Black signers of both genders mouth markedly less frequently than other signers.

FEATURES OF AFRICAN AMERICAN ENGLISH

We turn now to the incorporation of features of African American English into Black ASL. In a study of lexical variation, Aramburo (1989) has noted that some of the important features of Black ASL variation are related to facial expression and body movement. In a more extensive examination of the incorporation of AAE features into Black ASL, Lewis (1998) considers "whether there are elements of Ebonics in the sign language of African Americans" (229). Following a discussion of the features of AAE, Lewis analyzes the performed ASL narrative of one signer who makes what Lewis calls "Ebonic shifts," characterized by a marked rhythmic pattern, a side-to-side head movement, and a shift in body posture. He states that "If we consider these features in terms of Smitherman's tonal semantics [1977], we can see that rhythm does indeed add a 'songified' quality in the signer's signing" (236).

Lewis's data consist of a performance and are quite different from our recordings of people engaged in informal conversation and interviews. We cannot say that we have naturally occurring examples of the features that Lewis describes. We did collect examples of single words and phrases, as well as discussions of AAE features. All of the examples come from the signers under the age of 35, who by definition attended integrated schools. Given the advances in technology since the older signers were in school, these younger signers would also have had much more exposure to the use of AAE through movies and media of various kinds. Many of the examples (see the DVD) were produced during the interview portion of the filming in response to the following questions: "Do you think that Black signing is different from White signing? Do Black people sign differently from White people?"

In Alabama, the questions elicited a discussion of the sign TRIP and the phrase STOP TRIPPING. The handshape and movement for the sign are the same as for the lexical sign TRIP—crooked V handshape moving outward in a repeated arc—but the sign is produced at the forehead to indicate the cognitive component of the meaning (i.e., "stop imagining things"). It was also produced in this location simply with a short, repeated outward movement without the arc. A long discussion also focused on what appeared to be the phrase "What's up, n_____?" One participant clarified that the sign actually meant "nerd," so that the phrase was "What's up, nerd?" This participant stated that his White friends were alarmed to see the phrase until it was explained that the intended meaning was "nerd." The phrase STUPID FOOL was also briefly discussed as being a Black usage, and PLEASE appeared in a discussion about big city traffic: POWERFUL, WOW (gesture), PLEASE.

Often, in response to the interview questions, the younger participants demonstrated their perception of Black signing style by shifting their bodies markedly to one side, exaggerating the movement, and expanding the size of the signing space. This was the response in North Carolina, in which WHASSUP? was provided as an example of Black signing style. The handshape is the same as the lexical sign, open 8 handshape, and palm toward the chest, but the upward movement was slowed down and occupied a larger space. In Virginia, the body shift, exaggerated movement, and larger signing space were demonstrated as the signer responded to a question. Rather than offer a specific sign like WHASSUP, he responded: "Black signing, yes, it looks like this . . ." In addition, in North Carolina a phrase from AAE incorporated into Black ASL was spontaneously produced: At the end of a comment about attendance at the picnic where the filming was taking place, one young signer paused and then signed #DANG, a lexicalized fingerspelling of the English word "dang," first with her left hand and then with her right hand. She produced each one at waist level, well below the usual fingerspelling area in front of the shoulder, and moved her body forward for emphasis as she was signing.

By far the most examples of AAE incorporated into Black ASL occurred in a younger group from Houston, recorded shortly after the 2008 presidential election. During a long and lively discussion about Obama at the beginning of the free conversation, one participant responded, GIRL, PLEASE. During this discussion, all three of the participants repeatedly slapped 5 with each other in agreement about a point one of them was making; this slapping 5 was usually in the middle of a turn, not at the end. Often the participants were overlapping in their turn and continued with what they were saying after they slapped 5. The male participant in this group signed HELL at the end of a sentence for emphasis after having offered an opinion. Finally, in a discussion with the interviewer about Black signs, the participants signed and discussed the Black version of MY BAD, an S handshape with the palm down and contacting the upper chest in the same location as LAZY and

QUALIFIED, with repeated movement. One participant contrasted this to how White signers might sign it (i.e., MY and BAD in sequence, as opposed to the separate lexical item the Black signers used).

As chapter 4 points out, users of Black ASL recognize differences between Black signing and White signing, and Black signers incorporate lexical items, phrases, and gestures from AAE into their signing. In addition, as chapter 5 discusses, Black signers seem to endorse the common perception that Black ASL tends to use a larger signing space than does White ASL. Finally, although not conclusive, our data offer further evidence of language change. Older and younger Black signers differ in the extent to which they incorporate AAE lexical items into their signing, with younger signers using many more lexical items that originated in spoken AAE.

8

Lexical Variation

Lexical variation is, of course, one of the features that we must consider as we discuss whether we can characterize Black ASL as a distinct variety of ASL. Differences in the lexical choices of Black signers and White signers have been observed since 1965, when Croneberg contributed appendix D to William Stokoe's *Dictionary of American Sign Language,* discussed in chapter 1 of this volume. Somewhat later, Woodward, Erting, and Oliver (1976) examined a subset of signs that can all be produced either on the face or on the hands. They found that White signers produced more of the face variants than did Black signers. (We return to this study later in this chapter.) As we mentioned in chapter 5, Woodward and DeSantis (1977) found that two-handed signs such as CAT, COW, and FAMOUS can also be produced with one hand but that Black signers preferred the two-handed variants. Other studies that have explored lexical variation include Aramburo (1989), Guggenheim (1993), Lewis, Palmer, and Williams (1995), and Lewis (1998). More recently, Lucas, Bayley, Reed, and Wulf (2001) have looked at lexical differences between Black and White signers. Signers were shown twenty-six pictures and eight fingerspelled words to elicit their signs. For 28 of the 34 signs, the Black signers used signs that the White signers did not. The only six signs for which the Black signers did not have their own unique variants were CAKE, MICROWAVE, JAPAN, SANDWICH, THIEF, and STEAL. Furthermore, whereas White signers had fingerspelled variants of ARREST, BANANA, FEAR, and GLOVES, Black signers did not, but they did have fingerspelled variants of DEER and RABBIT. It was clear from this study that although Black signers and White signers share a lexicon, not all areas of it overlap.

We express our gratitude to Tiffany Braga, TaWanda Barkely, and Page Roberts, who contributed to this chapter in a substantial way.

In the present study, we look at what kind of lexical variation was spontaneously *produced* by the participants during the free conversation part of the filming. This is lexical variation produced that the participants did not comment on but the researchers noticed either while viewing the free conversation remotely as it was taking place or when they reviewed the data later. We then look at what kind of lexical variation the participants spontaneously *discussed* during the free conversation and also both observed remotely and noticed during the review of the data tapes. We then examine the participants' responses to three of the interview questions: (1) Can you think of specific signs that are different for Black signers and White signers? (2) Are there old signs that you don't see much anymore? (3) What are some signs that are unique to this area? We focused on what our participants spontaneously signed and talked about; thus, our discussion is not a systematic comparison of the signs used by Black signers and White signers in general. It may be the case that the signs that our participants produced and discussed are also those that White signers use. Finally, we reexamine Woodward, Erting, and Oliver's (1976) comparison of Black and White signers to get a sense of how it looks more than three decades later.

Lexical Variation Produced by the Participants

Tables 8.1 and 8.2 show the lexical variation the signers spontaneously produced during the free conversation. We see that most of it is produced by the older signers and that most of the signs relate to everyday life. It is evenly divided between the categories of nouns and verbs. Since these signs were produced during free conversation, the interviewer was not present to request explanation or clarification. The Virginia signers did not produce any examples, and only in Louisiana and Alabama did the younger signers produce any examples. It is interesting to note that two of the signs the younger signers produced, PICNIC and HOSPITAL, are signs known to have many variants. The Louisiana sign WATCH is also commonly used in Texas.

Table 8.1. Lexical Variation Spontaneously Produced by Signers over the Age of 55 during Free Conversation

State	Noun	Verb	Other
Alabama	none	TALK, TIGHT-LIP	SORE
Arkansas	FUNERAL	HAIR-PRESSING	none
Louisiana	SCHOOL, HIDE-AND-SEEK	HAIR-PRESSING, IN-STITUTE, HIDE-AND-SEEK, PEE	LIGHT-SKINNED
North Carolina	MIRACLE, THANKSGIVING, EASTER, ROLLS, UNDERWEAR	CAN'T-HELP, RUN (track), BLAME	YELLOW-SKIN NOT-FAIR,
Texas	none	WATCH	WRONG
Virginia	none	none	none

Table 8.2. Lexical Variation Spontaneously Produced by Signers under the Age of 35 during Free Conversation

State	Noun	Verb	Other
Alabama	HOSPITAL	none	none
Louisiana	PICNIC	WATCH	none

Figure 8.1. Variation produced, UNDERWEAR.

LEXICAL VARIATION SPONTANEOUSLY DISCUSSED
BY THE PARTICIPANTS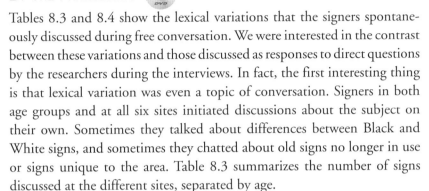

Tables 8.3 and 8.4 show the lexical variations that the signers spontaneously discussed during free conversation. We were interested in the contrast between these variations and those discussed as responses to direct questions by the researchers during the interviews. In fact, the first interesting thing is that lexical variation was even a topic of conversation. Signers in both age groups and at all six sites initiated discussions about the subject on their own. Sometimes they talked about differences between Black and White signs, and sometimes they chatted about old signs no longer in use or signs unique to the area. Table 8.3 summarizes the number of signs discussed at the different sites, separated by age.

In quantitative terms, a very clear difference is evident between the older and the younger signers. For instance, many of the examples from the older signers came from one Louisiana group in which the lexical variants spontaneously discussed ranged from BLACK and WHITE to days of the week, relationship signs such as FLIRT, SWEETHEART, BREAK-UP and signs for sports, with the participants showing the variants of these signs used when they were in school at the Southern School for the Deaf in Scotlandville. Lexical signs discussed in other groups include food (TOMATO, HOT DOG, CHICKEN) and school-related signs (SCHOOL, COACH, EDUCATION).

Table 8.3. Lexical Variation Discussed by Age and Site

State	Over 55	Under 35
Alabama	0	2
Arkansas	1	1
Louisiana	36	5
North Carolina	10	2
Texas	11	14
Virginia	2	0
Total	60	24

Figure 8.2a. SCHOOL (Louisiana).

Figure 8.2b. CHICKEN (Texas).

Figures 8.2a and 8.2b illustrate a New Orleans sign for SCHOOL and a Texas sign for CHICKEN, discussed by the older signers.

As table 8.4 shows, the older signers' discussion had a much wider semantic range than the younger signers'. This is probably because, as one participant observed, the older signers had signed differently when they were attending segregated schools and have had to learn new signs. This in contrast to younger signers, who attended integrated schools and have always had more of a shared lexicon with White signers. What is fascinating is that this difference emerges so clearly from the participants' casual conversations. One of the most interesting discussions occurred with the young group from Texas. Filmed just four days after the November 2008 presidential election, the whole free-conversation part of the interview centered on Obama and McCain, their positions, and, most interestingly,

Table 8.4. Lexical Variation Discussed by Age and Semantic Area

Semantic Area	Over 55	Under 35
Food	6	0
School	1	2
Sports	4	0
Places	3	2
People/relationships	12	18
Personal characteristics/feelings	9	2
Black vs. White	6	0
Miscellaneous	19	0
Total	60	24

the name signs the participants had noticed for each candidate. This group produced fourteen of the examples listed under "people/relationships" in table 8.4.

VARIATION DISCUSSED BY THE SIGNERS, RESPONSES TO INTERVIEW QUESTIONS

In this section we discuss the participants' responses to specific interview questions about lexical variation. The first question concerns differences between Black signs and White signs: "Do you think Black people sign differently from White people?"

It was easy for the participants to respond to this question and, not surprisingly, particularly easy for the older signers (see table 8.5).

The older signers often produced signs that were different from those used at the White school. They also produced older signs and compared them with newer signs, as the old ones have fallen out of use. In fact, the

Table 8.5. Signers' Responses to Interview Questions, Black vs. White

State	Over 55	Under 35
Alabama	0	22
Arkansas	22	10
Louisiana	37	7
North Carolina	30	7
Texas	31	4
Virginia	20	8
Total	140	58

older signers provided slightly more than two and one half times as many responses as the younger signers. The older signers commented repeatedly that the Black signs they were producing were ones that they had used in school but are no longer in use. The signs covered a wide range of semantic areas (see table 8.6).

Table 8.6. Semantic Areas in Response to Interview Questions, Black vs. White

Semantic Area	Over 55	Under 35
Food	25	7
School	5	3
Sports	2	1
Places names	11	3
People/relationships	9	5
Personal characteristics/feelings	12	4
Signs for BLACK and WHITE	6	5
Miscellaneous	70	30
Total	140	58

Food signs include CEREAL, SODA, CAKE, CORNBREAD, BISCUIT, CAB-BAGE, BEANS, and TEA. We observed variants for SCHOOL and GRADUATION and, in the area of sports, for BASKETBALL. Place name variants include GALVESTON, DALLAS, and FORT WORTH. For people and relationships, the

Figure 8.3a. STEAL (Louisiana).

Figure 8.3b. FLIRT (Louisiana).

participants produced variants for FLIRT, KISS, BOSS, FRIEND, GIRL-FRIEND, PRESIDENT, MOTHER, and BROTHER. DUMB, BORED, UGLY, TALL, and FAT illustrate variants in the personal characteristics and feelings area, and a number of signs that do not group naturally into one semantic area were shown, including HURT, NONE-OF-YOUR-BUSINESS, GO, and SUN. Figures 8.3a and 8.3b illustrate Black New Orleans signs for STEAL and FLIRT.

ARE THERE OLDER SIGNS THAT YOU DON'T SEE MUCH ANYMORE?

Next in the interview, we asked the project participants, "Are there older signs that you don't see much anymore?" We posed the question to both age groups. The older participants were asked to recall information from thirty to forty years ago.

When interviewed with their peers, participants over 55 who attended segregated schools were able to recall many specific older signs. They referred to them as "signs in the old days or old school signs." Some of the project participants under 30 could not recall the older signs, with the exception of those who were from Deaf families, who said their Deaf families still use some of the older signs. Some of the project participants said they attended the integrated schools and were not exposed to the older signs.

Tables 8.7 and 8.8 list the older signs that the project participants, both older and younger, recalled using at their schools.

The tables are divided into three categories: noun, verb, and other. We see different responses depending on the region: The older Louisiana, Arkansas, Texas, and Virginia participants showed us older signs for each category, while the North Carolina participants produced only nouns. As with other responses, the signs they produced have to do mainly with food and the home environment (i.e., everyday life). Figure 8.4 illustrates older Louisiana signs for the days of the week.

As table 8.8 shows, only the younger participants from North Carolina, Arkansas, and Virginia were able to remember a few of the older signs in

Table 8.7. Lexical Variation Discussed by Signers over the Age of 55, Older Signs

State	Noun	Verb	Other
Alabama	GUM, CORN, CORNBREAD, WATERMEL-ON, GREYHOUND BUS, TRUCK, SHOES, SLIP	LOOK	BROWN
Arkansas	SODA, POP, STORE, SHOES, CADILLAC, SQUIRREL	GRADUATE, LAUGH, WINK, WORK	WRONG, BLACK
Louisiana	BUSINESS, SCHOOL	BOSSY, KEEP, REMEM-BER, FORGOT, FLIRT, PEE	BORED, WITH
North Carolina	CORNFLAKE, SODA, CEREAL, BATH-ROOM, MOVIE, SUN, SAMBO (AFRICA), TOWEL, COLOR, SCIENCE, SEX	none	none
Texas	SCHOOL, BATH, SEX, RESTROOM	GONE, WAIT, SHARP, FINISH, SHIT	DAMN, NONE-OF-YOUR-BUSINESS
Virginia	APPLE, PEANUTS, POTATOES, ORANGE, CAKE, WATER, BATHROOM, SOCKS, COLOR, SQUIRREL, BIRTHDAY	FILMING, STEAL	LAZY, PREGNANT

Table 8.8. Lexical Variation Discussed by Signers under the Age of 35, Older Signs

State	Noun	Verb
Alabama	none	none
Arkansas	MOVIE, THING	STAY, HAVE
Louisiana	none	none
North Carolina	CORNBREAD, BOSS, BOOK, SCHOOL, PARTY	none
Texas	none	none
Virginia	SODA, BIRTHDAY, TRASH	none

the category of food, days of the week, school, home and community, and noun (other). Project participants from Alabama, Louisiana, and Texas could not recall any older signs.

Figure 8.4. DAYS OF THE WEEK (Louisiana).

What Are Some of the Signs Unique to This Area?

Finally, we asked whether the signers could produce any signs unique to their area. Table 8.9 reports the results from the younger signers. Again, the signs have to do with aspects of everyday life.

The younger signers seemed to understand the question, while the older ones seemed to assume they were being asked about signs they remembered using at their schools, such as the one illustrated in figure 8.5.

Revisiting an Earlier Study

As we mentioned at the beginning of this chapter, an early study of phonological variation in ASL by Woodward, Erting, and Oliver (1976) examined a subset of signs, including MOVIE, RABBIT, LEMON, COLOR, SILLY, PEACH, and PEANUT, which can all be produced either on the face or on the hands. They found that White signers produced more of the face variants than did Black signers. We decided to reexamine these results thirty-five years later. In contemporary ASL, MOVIE and RABBIT are most commonly produced as two-handed signs in neutral space; the older form of MOVIE is produced with a 5 handshape, palm facing in, either

Table 8.9. Lexical Variation Unique to Area

State	Signs
Alabama	PEANUT, GRAY, MOTHER, WHITE, TRUCK, NEVER-HEARD
Arkansas	none
North Carolina	TRUCK, HOSPITAL, STORE, TOWEL, CANDY, STRAWBERRY, GRAY, SUNDAY
Louisiana	CHEERLEADER, BIRTHDAY, WATCH, DONKEY
Texas	SOON, CHEAT, EXCUSE-ME, HELL, GRAY
Virginia	WINE, SUNDAY, CABBAGE, CHICKEN

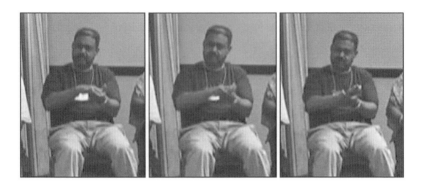

Figure 8.5. SHOES (Arkansas).

two-handed or one-handed. The contemporary form of SILLY is an oscil-
lating Y handshape produced in front of the face. The contemporary
forms of LEMON, COLOR, PEACH, and PEANUT are all produced on the face.
According to Woodward, Erting, and Oliver (1976), however, we should
expect the Black signers to produce more hand versions of these signs
than face versions. At the end of the interviews, we showed the participants pictures designed to elicit their signs for these seven items. We also
elicited the sign AFRICA, which was not in the original group, but we
included it because of its changing history. An old sign for AFRICA involves
an A handshape circling the face or circling the face and ending on the
nose. Both have been labeled offensive by Black signers. However, in
1987, in a performance of the play *KISSFEST,* one signer introduced a sign
made in neutral space that traced the outline of the continent with one
hand (N. Marbury, personal communication, June 25, 2010). The community has used this until fairly recently, when a number of African signers stated that they were quite happy with the A handshape circling the
face since it is very similar to the sign BEAUTIFUL. Both the newer sign and
the older sign are seen in the community now, but most of the older signers in our study do not use the newer one.

Tables 8.10–8.15 illustrate the results of this elicitation task, in which
66 of 76 signers participated. Some of the columns list two numbers. The

Table 8.10. North Carolina, Response to Lexical Elicitation

	Hand	Face	Notes
Under 35 (7 signers)			
RABBIT	7	0, 1	
COLOR	0	7, 3	Three signers mentioned the L handshape variety on the cheek.
LEMON	0, 3	7	Three signers mentioned the "old" variant.
PEACH	0	7	
PEANUT	0	7, 2	Two signers remembered the ear variant.
MOVIE	7	0, 1	One signer remembered the old face variant.
AFRICA	7	0, 4	Three signers mentioned the "old" sign.
Over 55 (8 signers)			
RABBIT	8	0	
COLOR	0	8, 5	One older signer produced only the L handshape on the face. Five others mentioned that sign as the "old" variant.
LEMON	3, 2	4	
PEACH	7, 1	1, 0	
PEANUT	0	8, 2	Two signers said the Raleigh school had a second variant on the nose.
MOVIE	2, 2	6, 2	
AFRICA	0, 4	7	All used the face variant first but said "some people use" the hand variant.

Note: When someone in the group had strong feelings about a particular sign, that person seemed to persuade the other signers toward it.

first represents the number of signers who produced a given sign as their first response; the second represents the number of signers who produced a given sign as their second response. So, in table 8.10, for example, in North Carolina, seven signers produced the on-the-hands version of RABBIT as their first response, while only one produced the head version as a second response.

In table 8.10, we see the responses for North Carolina, both for older and younger signers. In many cases, both younger and older signers show awareness of what they refer to as "older" forms like COLOR and MOVIE (see figures 8.6 and 8.7), be they produced on the hands or the face, while seeming to prefer the newer forms. The Arkansas signers in table 8.11 specifically mention differences between Black signs and White signs, as with COLOR, and specify an "ASL" variant of PEANUT. They also specify the face variant of MOVIE as older and hand variants of PEACH, LEMON, and COLOR as older. The older Texas signers in table 8.12 show hand variants of COLOR and LEMON, while the younger signers still prefer—or prefer again—the face variant of AFRICA. In table 8.13, we see that the younger Alabama signers show hand variants of PEACH, and one states that both the hand and face variants of PEANUT are acceptable. The older signers describe the face variants of MOVIE and RABBIT and the hand variant of COLOR as old signs. Three of the younger Virginia signers state that the face variant of AFRICA is offensive. The older Virginia signers still use a hand variant of PEACH and mention older versions of RABBIT (face) and COLOR (hands). Louisiana signers in table 8.15 show both variants of RABBIT, and the older signers agree that the face variant of AFRICA is no longer appropriate.

All of the signers, then, show awareness of the older forms of signs that Woodward, Erting, and Oliver (1976) described. Specifically in terms of the claim that Black signers use more of the hand variants than do White signers, the overall results are summarized in table 8.16.

Figure 8.6. COLOR.

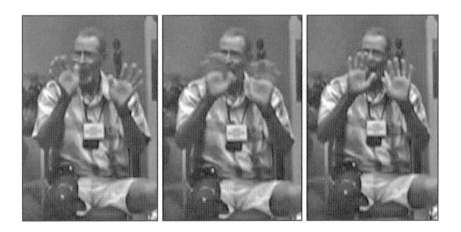

Figure 8.7. MOVIE.

Table 8.11. Arkansas, Response to Lexical Elicitation

	Hand	Face	Notes
Under 35 (3 signers)			
RABBIT	3	0, 2	Two signers mentioned the old sign on the face.
COLOR	0, 1	3	One signer remembered the old hand variant.
LEMON	2	1, 2	Two said the old sign was on the hands.
PEACH	2	1, 2	Two signers first signed the hand variant but also remembered the face sign.
PEANUT	0	3	Signed on teeth. Had never seen cheek variant.
MOVIE	0, 2	2	Two signers remembered the old sign at the face. One signer signed WATCH.
AFRICA	1, 2	2	Two signers first used the face variant but said they had learned the hand sign.
Over 55 (11 signers)			
RABBIT	10, 1	1, 5	One signer gave the face variant, and five others agreed that that was the old sign.
COLOR	0, 9	11	Four signers said the hand variant was the old sign and that the new sign is the "White" sign. Others said the old way was to fingerspell.
LEMON*	4, 5	6	Signers agreed that the hand variant was the old sign.

(Continued on next page)

	Hand	Face	Notes
PEACH**	6	0, 4	Six signers agreed on the old sign, but four also produced the face variant as their current sign.
PEANUT	2	9, 1	All signers said the old sign was articulated at the cheek but that the ASL sign is on the teeth.
MOVIE	4, 2	7, 2	Seven signers produced the face variant first as the old sign. Two others also remembered that sign.
AFRICA	0, 6	11	All signers gave the old sign on the face but agreed that you're "now supposed to" sign the hand variant.

Note: In this group the two males seemed a bit older than the female. She didn't remember older variants that they mentioned.

* One signer didn't produce a sign for LEMON.

** Four signers never produced the sign PEACH because they thought that the picture was an apple.

Table 8.12. Texas, Response to Lexical Elicitation

	Hand	Face	Notes
Under 35 (3 signers)			
RABBIT	3	0	
COLOR	0	3	
LEMON	0	3	
PEACH	0	3	
PEANUT	0	3	
MOVIE	3	0	
AFRICA	0, 3	3	All signers noted the hand variant but preferred the face variant.
Over 55 (2 signers)			
COLOR	0, 1	2	Signer showed the old sign to be on the hands.
LEMON	0, 1	2	One signer mentioned that the old way was to fingerspell L-E-M-O-N.
PEACH	0	2	
peanut	0, 1	2	Signer said her father signed PEANUT on the hands.
MOVIE	1	1	
AFRICA	0, 1	2	One signer mentioned the hand variant.

Table 8.13. Alabama, Response to Lexical Elicitation

	Hand	Face	Notes
Under 35 (6 signers)			
RABBIT	6	0, 3	One signer signed both variants. Another said the face variant is the old sign.
COLOR	0	6	
LEMON	0	6	
PEACH	1	5, 1	One signer first signed this on his hands, then moved it to his face.
PEANUT	1, 1	5	One signer said either variant is fine.
MOVIE	6	0	
AFRICA	5, 1	1, 3	All signers agreed that the sign on the face is the old variant.
Over 55 (4 signers)			
RABBIT	4	0, 1	One signer said the face variant is the "old" sign.
COLOR	0, 2	4	Two signers said the hand variant is the old sign.
LEMON	0	4	
PEACH	0, 1	4	One signer said "some people sign" the hand variant.
PEANUT	4	0	
MOVIE	4	0	One signer offered the "old" variant in front of the face.
AFRICA	0	4	

Table 8.14. Virginia, Response to Lexical Elicitation

	Hand	Face	Notes
Under 35 (4 signers)			
RABBIT	4	0	
COLOR	0	4	
LEMON	0	4	
PEACH	4	0, 1	One signer mentioned the hand variant.
PEANUT	0	4	On teeth.
MOVIE	4	0	
AFRICA	4	0, 3	Three signers mentioned the old sign but said that it was offensive.
Over 55 (7 signers)			
RABBIT	7	0, 4	Four signers mentioned the old sign on the face.
COLOR	0, 3	7	All of the signers produced a sign on the face. Three mentioned an old sign on the hands.
LEMON	1	6, 1	One signer said she used to fingerspell the word but now uses an L at the chin. Also, three different variants for the signs on the face were produced.
PEACH	5	0	Two signers first mentioned that they used to fingerspell P-E-A-C-H but now have the hand sign.
PEANUT	0	7, 1	At ear. One signer mentioned the new sign at the ear with shock.
MOVIE	0	7	
AFRICA	0, 1	6	

Note: All signers gave both the 5 hand and the L hand signs for color.

Table 8.15. Louisiana, Response to Lexical Elicitation

	Hand	Face	Notes
Under 35 (6 signers)			
RABBIT	4	2	Both females used the face variant. All males used the hand variant.
COLOR	0	6	
LEMON	0	6	
PEACH	0	6	
PEANUT	0	6	
MOVIE	6	0	
AFRICA	3, 2	3, 1	
Over 55 (5 signers)			
RABBIT	2, 1	3, 2	Two signers produced the hand sign first and then agreed that the face sign was the old variant.
COLOR	0, 3	5	
LEMON	0, 2	5	
PEACH	0	2	Three signers fingerspelled P-E-A-C-H.
PEANUT	2, 1	3, 1	
movie	4	1, 2	
AFRICA	1, 3	4	All signers agreed that the face variant is no longer appropriate.

Table 8.16. Summary of Hand Variants: First Response to Elicitation

Sign	North Carolina		Arkansas		Texas		Alabama		Virginia		Louisiana		Total	
	−35	55+	−35	55+	−35	55+	−35	55+	−35	55+	−35	55+	−35	55+
RABBIT	7/7	8/8	3/3	10/11	3/3	2/2	6/6	4/4	4/4	7/7	4/6	2/5	27/29	33/37
COLOR	0/7	0/8	0/3	0/11	0/3	0/2	0/6	0/4	0/4	0/7	0/6	0/5	0/29	0/37
LEMON	0/7	3/8	2/3	4/11	0/3	0/2	0/6	0/4	0/4	1/7	0/6	0/5	2/29	8/37
PEACH	0/7	7/8	2/3	2/11	0/3	0/2	1/6	0/4	4/4	5/7	0/6	0/5	7/29	14/37
PEANUT	0/7	0/8	0/3	2/11	0/3	0/2	1/6	4/4	0/4	0/7	0/6	2/5	1/29	8/37
MOVIE	7/7	2/8	0/3	4/11	3/3	1/2	6/6	4/4	4/4	0/7	6/6	4/5	26/29	15/37
AFRICA	7/7	0/8	1/3	0/11	0/3	2/2	5/6	0/4	4/4	0/7	3/6	1/5	20/29	3/37

We see here how many signers produced the hand variant of a sign as their *first* response. This table can be summarized as follows:

RABBIT: The hand variant still used (but it is probably the most used variant by White signers also; the older sign produced on the head has no doubt been subjected to the centralization described earlier.

COLOR: The first responses are all face variants.

LEMON: The first responses are almost all face variants.

PEACH: Only one-quarter of the young signers produce the hand variant as their first response; 14/37 older signers produce the hand variant first.

MOVIE: The young signers mostly use the hand variant (also no doubt the result of centralization); almost half of the older signers still use the older face variant.

In some cases—COLOR and LEMON—neither the older nor the younger signers produce the hand variants. Younger signers do not produce the hand variants of PEACH and PEANUT, while older signers still produce some. The hand variants of MOVIE and RABBIT are newer variants by virtue of centralization, and that is what the younger signers produce. So it would appear that we see some language change from 1976, when Woodward, Erting, and Oliver observed that Black signers use more of the hand variants than do White signers. Except for MOVIE and RABBIT, the younger signers no longer produce the hand variants even though they may be aware of those older forms.

As for AFRICA, almost all of the younger signers produce the newer hand variant, while almost all of the older signers produce the A-on-the-face variant. It will be interesting to watch the progress of this sign to see whether there is a return to the older face variant as a result of attitudes about the new variant.

Summary

So we see that signers spontaneously produced lexical variation in free conversation and also discussed it, sometimes at great length. Lexical variation is obviously quite available as a topic of conversation. The participants in this study are quite aware of lexical differences between themselves and White signers and can easily recall older signs, often those that they used when they were in school together. In fact, older signs and their use are a central part of the memories of these older signers. Moreover, we see lexical change in progress as younger signers may be aware of but do not use the hand variants observed by Woodward, Erting, and Oliver in 1976. Lexical variation, then, is a key feature in distinguishing Black ASL as a distinct variety.

9

Conclusions

We come back now to the questions that we ask in chapter 1. First, we ask what sociohistorical reality would lead to the development of a separate variety such as Black ASL. Chapter 2 offers an overview of the history of education for Black deaf children and of our six sites. In this history of segregated schools, we can clearly see the geographical and social isolation that would make a separate language variety possible. We see the obvious effects of the discrimination and oppression that were integral to the pre–civil rights South. We also see how the sociohistorical reality has changed and is continuing to change with school integration and then mainstreaming. The information we present in chapter 2 is reflected in the perceptions of the participants in our study, both older and younger, as we see in chapter 4. Older signers reflect very poignantly on their experiences in the schools and departments for Black deaf children, while younger signers talk about their experiences in integrated schools.

On the basis of previous research and our own observations of the data for this and earlier studies, we suggest that Black ASL might well be characterized by a range of features at different linguistic levels. Table 9.1 lists the features under investigation and summarizes our results.

In the area of phonology, we find that Black signers tended to use older, more traditional forms than their White counterparts. In the case of two-handed signs that can also be produced with one hand, the signers in our study chose the two-handed variant in more than 65 percent of the tokens we analyzed. In the case of signs produced at the forehead level (in citation form) that can be lowered, the Black signers in this study selected the nonlowered variant in 70 percent of the tokens analyzed. Black signers,

Table 9.1. Summary of Results for the Linguistic Variables

Feature Type	Feature	Data Analyzed	Results
phonology	variation between one-handed and two-handed signs	818 tokens from free conversations, interviews, and NBDA conversations	Black signers use more two-handed variants than White signers, and older Black signers use more two-handed variants than younger Black signers.
	location of signs such as KNOW	877 tokens from free conversations, interviews, and NBDA conversations	Black signers use more non-lowered variants than White signers, and older Black signers use more nonlowered variants than younger Black signers.
	size of the signing space in Black and White ASL	2,247 tokens from elicited and free narratives	Black signers use a larger signing space than White signers; however, younger White signers have converged with younger Black signers.
syntax	clausal or phrasal repetition	26 ten-minute conversations	Black signers make greater use of repetition than White signers.

discourse and pragmatics	constructed dialogue and constructed action	24 elicited narratives; 21 free narratives	Black signers appear to use more constructed action and constructed dialogue; however, the data show a great deal of individual variation. Further research is needed.
contact with English	mouthing of English	26 ten-minute conversations	Older Black signers appear to mouth less than other signers; however, further research is necessary.
contact with AAE (lexical, phrasal)	borrowing of expressions from AAE (e.g., "girl," "my bad")	examples spontaneously produced in interviews and free conversations	Black signers incorporate AAE lexical items into their signing. Younger Black signers incorporate more AAE lexical items than their elders.
lexicon	differences in Black and White signs for common items and concepts (e.g., MOVIE, COLOR, RABBIT, AFRICA)	spontaneously produced examples, spontaneously discussed signs, and responses to specific interview questions	Lexical variation persists, but younger Black signers use fewer "Black" variants than their elders.

particularly the older ones, also use a larger signing space than do the White signers. We refer to these as older, more traditional forms because we know from other researchers that processes of centralization—for lowered signs and smaller signing space—and reduction (for two-handed signs)—have been ongoing in ASL. Frishberg (1975) describes the reduction of two-handed signs and centralization processes, while Liddell and Johnson (1989) also describe the centralization of signs. In the areas of syntax and discourse, we find that Black signers use much more repetition of single lexical items and phrases than do White signers and that the older signers appear to use more constructed dialogue. The older Black signers also do markedly less mouthing, and there are many lexical differences, which are to be expected.

So the sociohistorical reality characterized by geographically and socially isolated residential schools have indeed led to the development of a distinct variety of ASL, as we see with the older signers, a variety characterized by, among other things, more two-handed signs, more forehead-level signs, a larger signing space, more repetition, possibly more constructed dialogue, less mouthing, and lexical differences. We say "among other things" because these are the linguistic features that we have focused on; there may be others that remain to be analyzed. However, with integration and mainstreaming, that reality has been changing, and the language reflects those changes. Younger Black signers still use more two-handed and forehead-level signs and repetition than White signers, but the signing space that young White signers use is similar to that of young Black signers. In comparing young Black signers and young White signers, we find no significant differences in the amount of mouthing. There are still lexical differences, and young Black signers incorporate African American English into their signing in ways that White signers do not.

In chapter 1 we ask whether the same kind of unique features that have been identified for African American English (AAE) are also pertinent to Black ASL. The answer is yes and no. In AAE, we observe linguistic features that do not appear in any White dialects, especially in the tense-aspect system. For example, AAE makes use of "invariant *be*" to indicate habitual action, as in "She always be in school." In addition, AAE uses the aspectual marker BIN to indicate that an event that happened in the past is still relevant, as in the sentence, "She BIN married," meaning she was married a long time ago and she is still married. However, in AAE we also observe many features of White dialects that may simply appear more frequently in AAE. For example, negative concord (or multiple negation, e.g., "I don't got none") is widespread in vernacular English dialects; however, it is used at a very high rate in AAE. In a similar way, the absence of the third-person singular verbal suffix /s/ (e.g., "Here come Johnny") is common in vernacular English dialects not only in the United States but also in other English-speaking countries; however, it is more common in AAE than in many other dialects.

Thus far, we have not identified unique features of Black ASL other than the incorporation of AAE and lexical items (and we saw markedly less spontaneously produced lexical variation among the younger Black signers). That is, White signers also produce one-handed versions of two-handed signs, lower signs that are produced at the forehead, and use a signing space that extends beyond the usual limit. White signers also use repetition, mouthing, and constructed action and constructed dialogue. Thus far, then, the differences between Black ASL and White ASL are quantitative rather than qualitative. However, in sharp contrast to the perceptions of the project participants presented in chapter 4—that White signing is "more advanced" and "better"—we find that this is simply not the case. As we see in the forms still used by the older signers but also used by the younger signers, Black ASL is in some respects more standard than White ASL if by "standard" we mean forms that have not undergone processes of change such as reduction and lowering and that, in the case of no mouthing, show dramatically less influence by spoken English.

We close with ideas for future research. One is, of course, to expand the present study beyond the six sites where we collected data to see what is happening in Georgia, Florida, Mississippi, and the northern states and in the process to greatly expand the pool of signers and thus the data available for comparison. Also, as mentioned earlier, we may have overlooked other linguistic features that it would be useful to analyze. Finally, in the course of doing this project, we have become aware of many Black Deaf families in the United States, families in which signing was and has always been the primary means of communication. This large network of families is definitely deserving of a full and systematic description, as are many aspects of the Black Deaf community in the United States and elsewhere. We hope that this project will serve as a model for the study and preservation of the history and heritage of other communities.

References

Adair, A. V. 1984. *Desegregation: The Illusion of Black Progress.* Lanham, Md.: University Press of America.

Ajello, R., L. Mazzoni, and F. Nicolai. 2001. Linguistic Gestures: Mouthing in Italian Sign Language (LIS). In P. Boyes Braem and R. Sutton-Spence, eds., *The Hands Are the Head of the Mouth,* 231–48. Hamburg: Signum.

Alabama Institute for the Deaf and Blind (AIDB). 1892. Annual Report. Talladega: Author.

———. 1894. Annual Report. Talladega: Author.

——— Archives. 1967, 1968, 1969.

Anderson, G. B. 2006. *Still I Rise: The Enduring Legacy of Black Deaf Arkansans before and after Integration.* Little Rock: Arkansas Association of the Deaf.

Andrews, J., and D. Jordan. 1993. Minority and Minority Deaf Professionals. *American Annals of the Deaf* 138: 388–96.

Aramburo, A. 1989. Sociolinguistic Aspects of the Black Deaf Community. In C. Lucas, ed., *The Sociolinguistics of the Deaf Community,* 103–22. New York: Academic Press.

Baer, A. M., A. Okrent, and M. Rose. 1996. Noticing Variation in ASL: Metalinguistic Knowledge and Language Attitudes across Racial and Regional Lines. In L. Byers and M. Rose, eds., *Communication Forum,* 1–33. Washington, D.C.: School of Communication, Gallaudet University.

Bailey, G. 2002. Apparent Time. In J. K. Chambers, P. Trudgill, and N. Schilling-Estes, eds., *The Handbook of Language Variation and Change,* 312–32. Oxford: Blackwell.

Bardes, A. P. 1952. The Alabama School for Negro Deaf. *The Silent Worker* (June).

Barnes, S. L. 2003. The Ebonics Enigma: An Analysis of Attitudes on an Urban College Campus. *Race, Ethnicity, and Education* 6: 247–63.

Bass, R. A. 1949. *History of the Education of the Deaf in Virginia 1839–1948.* Staunton: Virginia School for the Deaf and the Blind.

Battison, R. 1974. Phonological Deletion in American Sign Language. *Sign Language Studies* 5: 1–19.

———. 1978. *Lexical Borrowing in American Sign Language.* Silver Spring, Md.: Linstok.

Baugh, J. 1996. Perceptions within a Variable Paradigm: Black and White Detection and Identification Based on Speech. In E. W. Schneider, ed., *Focus on the USA,* 169–82. Amsterdam: Benjamins.

———. 2000. *Beyond Ebonics: Linguistic Pride and Racial Prejudice.* New York: Oxford University Press.

———. 2003. Linguistic Profiling. In S. Makoni, G. Smitherman, A. F. Ball, and A. K. Spears, eds., *Black Linguistics: Language, Society, and Politics in Africa and the Americas,* 155–68. London: Routledge.

———. 2007. Attitudes towards Variations and Ear-witness Testimony: Linguistic Profiling and Voice Discrimination in the Quest for Fair Housing and Fair Lending. In R. Bayley and C. Lucas, eds., *Sociolinguistic Variation: Theories, Methods, and Applications,* 338–48. New York: Cambridge University Press.

Bayley, R. 2002. The Quantitative Paradigm. In J. K. Chambers, P. Trudgill, and N. Schilling-Estes, eds., *The Handbook of Language Variation and Change,* 117–41.Oxford: Blackwell.

———, and C. Lucas. In press a. Phonological Variation in ASL in Louisiana ASL: An Exploratory Study. In M. Picone and C. E. Davies, eds., *Language Variety in the South: Historical and Contemporary Perspectives.* Tuscaloosa: University of Alabama Press.

———.In press b. Sign Languages. In R. Mesthrie, ed., *The Cambridge Handbook of Sociolinguistics.* New York: Cambridge University Press.

———, and M. Rose. 2000. Variation in American Sign Language: The Case of DEAF. *Journal of Sociolinguistics* 4: 81–107.

———. 2002. Phonological Variation in American Sign Language: The Case of 1 Handshape. *Language Variation and Change* 14: 19–53.

Baynton, D. C. 1996. *Forbidden Signs: American Culture and the Campaign against Sign Language.* Chicago: University of Chicago Press.

Bell, A. 1984. Language Style as Audience Design. *Language in Society* 13: 145–204.

———. 2001. Back in Style: Reworking Audience Design. In P. Eckert and J. R. Rickford, eds., *Style and Sociolinguistic Variation,* 139–69. New York: Cambridge University Press.

Bergman, B., and L. Wallin. 2001. A Preliminary Analysis of Visual Mouth Segments. In P. Boyes Braem and R. Sutton-Spence, eds., *The Hands Are the Head of the Mouth,* 51–68. Hamburg: Signum.

Bergmann, A., K. C. Hall, and S. Ross, eds. 2007. *Language Files,* 10th ed. Columbus: Ohio State University Press.

Berman, R., and D. I. Slobin, eds. 1994. *Relating Events in Narrative: A Cross-linguistic Study.* Hillsdale, N.J.: Erlbaum.

Bevill, R. E., and L. Vollmar. 1975. *History of the Arkansas School for the Deaf 1850–1975: 125th Anniversary of History of Education Services.* Little Rock: Arkansas School for the Deaf.

Boyd-Franklin, N., and A. J. Franklin. 2000. *Boys into Men: Raising Our African American Teenage Sons.* New York: Dutton.

Boyes Braem, P. 2001. Functions of the Mouthings in the Signing of Deaf Early and Late Learners of Swiss German Sign Language (DSGS). In P. Boyes Braem and R. Sutton-Spence, eds., *The Hands Are the Head of the Mouth,* 99–132. Hamburg: Signum.

———, and R. Sutton-Spence, eds. 2001. *The Hands Are the Head of the Mouth.* Hamburg: Signum.

Bradford, W. L. 1943. Work at the Louisiana State School for Negro Deaf. *American Annals of the Deaf* 88: 302–307.

Brentari, D. 1998. *A Prosodic Model of Sign Language Phonology.* Cambridge, Mass.: MIT Press.

———, ed. 2010. *Sign Languages.* New York: Cambridge University Press.

Brewer, J. M. 1935/1970. *Negro Legislators of Texas and Their Descendants.* Dallas: Mathis; 2nd ed. (1970), Austin: Jenkins.

Brill, R. G. 1950. The Training of Academic Teachers of the Deaf. PhD diss., Rutgers University.

Brown vs. Board of Education of Topeka, Kansas, U.S. 583 (1954).

Bucholtz, M. 1999. "Why Be Normal?" Language and Identity Practices in a Community of Nerd Girls. *Language in Society* 28: 203–23.

Burch, S. 2002. *Signs of Resistance: American Deaf Cultural History 1900–1942.* New York: New York University Press.

———, and H. Joyner. 2007. *Unspeakable: The Story of Junius Wilson.* Chapel Hill: University of North Carolina Press.

Cohen, O. P., J. Fischgrund, and R. Redding. 1990. Deaf Children from Ethnic, Linguistic, and Racial Minority Backgrounds. *American Annals of the Deaf* 135: 67–73.

Collins, S. C. 2004. Adverbial Morphemes in Tactile American Sign Language. PhD diss., Union Institute.

———, and K. Petronio. 1998. What Happens in Tactile ASL? In C. Lucas, ed., *Pinky Extension and Eye Gaze: Language Use in Deaf Communities,* 18–37. Washington, D.C.: Gallaudet University Press.

Crockett, M. H., and B. Crockett-Dease. 1990. *Through the Years 1867–1977. Light out of Darkness: A History of the North Carolina School for the Negro Blind and Deaf.* Raleigh: Barefeet Press.

Croneberg, C. 1965. Appendix D: Sign Language Dialects. In W. C. Stokoe, D. C Casterline, and C. G. Croneberg, *A Dictionary of American Sign Language,* 313–19. Silver Spring, Md.: Linstok.

Crouch, R., and J. Hawkins. 1983. *Out of Silence and Darkness: A History of the Alabama Institute for the Deaf and Blind.* Troy, Ala.: Troy State University Press.

Davis, J. 1989. Distinguishing Language Contact Phenomena in ASL Interpretation. In C. Lucas, ed., *The Sociolinguistics of the Deaf Community,* 85–102. San Diego: Academic.

Doctor, P. V. 1948. Deaf Negroes Get a Break in Education. *The Silent Worker* (November).

Dudis, P. 2002. Grounded Blend Maintenance as a Discourse Strategy. In C. Lucas, ed., *Turn-taking, Fingerspelling, and Contact in Signed Languages,* 53–73. Washington, D.C.: Gallaudet University Press.

———. 2004. Body Partitioning and Real-space Blends. *Cognitive Linguistics* 15: 223–38.

Dunn, L. 1995. Education, Culture, and Community: The Black Deaf Experience. In M. Garretson, ed., *Deafness: Life and Culture II. A Deaf*

American Monograph, vol. 45, 37–41. Silver Spring, Md.: National Association of the Deaf.

Ebbinghaus, H., and J. Hessmann. 2001. Sign Language as Multidimensional Communication: Why Manual Signs, Mouthings, and Mouth Gestures Are Three Different Things. In P. Boyes Braem and R. Sutton-Spence, eds., *The Hands Are the Head of the Mouth,* 133–52. Hamburg: Signum.

Eckert, P. 2000. *Linguistic Variation as Social Practice.* Oxford: Blackwell.

———, and S. McConnell-Ginet. 1992. Think Practically and Look Locally: Language and Gender as Community-based Practice. *Annual Review of Anthropology* 21: 461–90.

Edwards, W. F. 2008. African American Vernacular English: Phonology. In E. Schneider, ed., *Varieties of English.* Vol. 2, *The Americas and the Caribbean,* 181–91. Berlin: de Gruyter.

Emmorey, K. 1999. The Confluence of Space and Language in Signed Languages. In P. Bloom, M. A. Peterson, L. Nadel, and M. F. Garrett, eds., *Language and Space,* 171–209. Cambridge, Mass.: MIT Press.

———, and H. Lane, eds. 2000. *The Signs of Language Revisited: An Anthology to Honor Ursula Bellugi and Edward Klima.* Mahwah, N.J.: Erlbaum.

Fay, E. A. 1893. *Histories of American Schools for the Deaf, 1817–1893.* Washington, D.C.: Volta Bureau.

Finkelman, P. 2002. *Segregation in the United States.* http://www.mywire.com/a/Africana/Segregation-United-States/9446863/. Accessed November 23, 2010.

Flowers, T. 1915. Education of the Colored Deaf. In *Proceedings of the Twentieth Convention of American Instructors of the Deaf, 1914.* Washington, D.C.: U.S. Government Printing Office.

Fordham, S. 1999. Dissin' "the Standard": Ebonics as Guerrilla Warfare at Capital High. *Anthropology and Education Quarterly* 30: 272–93.

Frankenberg, E., and C. Lee. 2002. *Race in American Public Schools: Rapidly Resegregating School Districts.* http://civilrightsproject.ucla.edu/research/k-12-education/integration-and-diversity/race-in-american-public-schools-rapidly-resegregating-school-districts (accessed November 22, 2010).

Franklin, V. P. 1990. They Rose and Fell Together: African-American Educators and Community Leadership, 1795–1954. *Journal of Education* 172: 39–64.

Frazer, T. C. Attitudes toward Regional Pronunciation. *Journal of English Linguistics* 20(1): 89–100.

Frishberg, N. 1975. Arbitrariness and Iconicity: Historical Change in American Sign Language. *Language* 51: 696–719.

Fusfeld, I. S. 1941. Summer Courses for Teachers of the Deaf in Louisiana. *American Annals of the Deaf* 86: 385.

Galvan, D., and S. Taub. 2004. The Encoding of Motion Information in American Sign Language. In S. Strömqvist and L. Verhoeven, eds., *Relating Events in Narrative.* Vol. 2, *Typological and Contextual Perspectives,* 191–217. Mahwah, N.J.: Erlbaum.

Gannon, J. R. 1981. *Deaf Heritage: A Narrative History of Deaf America.* Silver Spring, Md.: National Association of the Deaf.

Garretson, M. 1980. Foreword. In C. Baker and R. Battison, eds., *Sign Language and the Deaf Community,* v–vi. Silver Spring, Md.: National Association of the Deaf.

Giles, H. 1973. Accent Mobility: A Model and Some Data. *Anthropological Linguistics* 15: 87–105.

———. 2001. Couplandia and Beyond. In P. Eckert and J. R. Rickford, eds., *Style and Sociolinguistic Variation,* 211–19. New York: Cambridge University Press.

———, and P. F. Powesland. 1975. *Speech Style and Social Evaluation.* London: Academic.

Graham, P. A. 1987. Black Teachers: A Drastically Scare Resource. *Phi Delta Kappan* 68: 598–605.

Green, L. 2002. *African American English: A Linguistic Introduction.* New York: Cambridge University Press.

———. 2004. Research on African American English since 1998. *Journal of English Linguistics* 32: 210–29.

Gruver, E. A. 1931 (September). President's Address. *American Annals of the Deaf* 76: 367–68.

Guggenheim, L. 1993. Ethnic Variation in ASL: The Signing of African Americans and How It Is Influenced by Topic. In E. Winston, ed., *Communication Forum,* 51–76. Washington, D.C.: School of Communication, Gallaudet University.

Hairston, E., and L. Smith. 1983. *Black and Deaf in America: Are We That Different?* Silver Spring, Md.: TJ Publishers.

Hearing Loss. http://www.4hearingloss.com/archives/2008/05/school_for_deaf_12.html (accessed September 24, 2010).

Higgins, F. C., and P. V. Doctor, comps. 1951. Tabular Statement of American Schools for the Deaf, Oct. 31, 1950. A.: Public Residential Schools in the United States. *American Annals of the Deaf* 96: 191–95.

Higgins, P. 1987. *Outsiders in a Hearing World: A Sociology of Deafness.* Beverly Hills: Sage.

Hill, J. Forthcoming. Language Attitudes and Perceptions in the American Deaf Community. PhD diss., Gallaudet University, Washington, D.C.

History of the Negro Department at the Tennessee School for the Deaf. 100th Anniversary of the History of the Tennessee School, 1845–1945. Tennessee School for the Deaf.

Hohenberger, A., and D. Happ. 2001. The Linguistic Primacy of Signs and Mouth Gestures over Mouthings: Evidence from Language Production in German Sign Language (DGS). In P. Boyes Braem and R. Sutton-Spence, eds., *The Hands Are the Head of the Mouth,* 153–90. Hamburg: Signum.

Hoopes, R., M. Rose, R. Bayley, C. Lucas, S. Collins, and K. Petronio. 2001. Analyzing Variation in Sign Languages: Theoretical and Methodological Issues. In V. Dively, M. Metzger, S. Taub, and A. M. Baer, eds. *Signed Languages: Discoveries from International Research,* 135–62. Washington, D.C.: Gallaudet University Press.

Houston Daily Union. 1871 (March 22). Gov. Holden in Washington: His Future Course Undecided: The Legislative Proceedings Said to Be Illegal.

Jia, L., and R. Bayley. 2002. Null Pronoun Variation in Mandarin Chinese. *University of Pennsylvania Working Papers in Linguistics* 8(3): 103–16.

Jowers, S. 2005. Ending the Educational Exile of Black Deaf Children from Washington, D.C.: *Miller v. Board of Education of the District of Columbia.* PhD diss., Howard University.

Kannapell, B. 1989. An Examination of Deaf College Students' Attitudes toward ASL and English. In C. Lucas, ed., *The Sociolinguistics of the Deaf Community,* 191–210. San Diego: Academic Press.

Keller, J. 2001. Multimodal Representations and the Linguistic Status of Mouthings in German Sign Language (DGS). In P. Boyes Braem and R. Sutton-Spence, eds., *The Hands Are the Head of the Mouth,* 191–230. Hamburg: Signum.

King, S. H. 1993. The Limited Presence of African American Teachers. *Review of Educational Research* 63: 115–49.

Labov, W. 1972a. *Language in the Inner City: Studies in the Black English Vernacular.* Philadelphia: University of Pennsylvania Press.

———. 1972b. *Sociolinguistic Patterns.* Philadelphia: University of Pennsylvania Press.

———. 1984. Field Methods of the Project on Language Variation and Change. In J. Baugh and J. Sherzer, eds., *Language in Use: Readings in Sociolinguistics,* 28–53. Englewood Cliffs, N.J.: Prentice Hall.

Lane, H., R. Hoffmeister, and B. Bahan. 1996. *A Journey into the DEAF-WORLD.* San Diego: DawnSignPress.

Lave, J., and E. Wenger. 1991. *Situated Learning: Legitimate Peripheral Participation.* New York: Cambridge University Press.

Lewis, J. 1998. Ebonics in American Sign Language: Stylistic Variation in African American Signers . In C. Carroll, ed., *Deaf Studies V: Toward 2000: Unity and Diversity.* Conference proceedings, April 17–20, 1997, 229–40. Washington, D.C.: College for Continuing Education, Gallaudet University.

———, C. Palmer, and L. Williams. 1995. Existence of and Attitudes toward Black Variations of Sign Language. In L. Byers, J. Chaiken, and M. Mueller, eds., *Communication Forum 1995,* 17–48. Washington, D.C.: School of Communication, Gallaudet University.

Liddell, S., and R. E. Johnson. 1989. American Sign Language: The Phonological Base. *Sign Language Studies* 64: 195–278.

Lippi-Green, R. 1997. *English with an Accent: Language, Ideology, and Discrimination in the United States.* London: Routledge.

Logan, Rayford W., and M. R. Winston, eds. 1982. *Dictionary of American Negro Biography.* New York: Norton.

Lucas, C. 1995. Sociolinguistic Variation in ASL: The Case of DEAF. In C. Lucas, ed., *Sociolinguistics in Deaf Communities,* 3–25. Washington, D.C.: Gallaudet University Press.

———, and Bayley, R. 2005. Variation in ASL: The Role of Grammatical Function. *Sign Language Studies* 6: 38–75.

———. 2010. Variation in ASL. In D. Brentari, ed., *Sign Languages,* 454–78. New York: Cambridge University Press.

———, R. Reed, and A. Wulf. 2001. Lexical Variation in African American and White Signing. *American Speech* 76: 339–60.

Lucas, C., R. Bayley, M. Rose, and A. Wulf. 2002. Location Variation in American Sign Language. *Sign Language Studies* 2: 407–40.

Lucas, C., R. Bayley, and C. Valli. 2001. *Sociolinguistic Variation in American Sign Language.* Washington, D.C.: Gallaudet University Press.

———. 2003. *What's Your Sign for PIZZA? An Introduction to Variation in American Sign Language.* Washington, D.C.: Gallaudet University Press.

Lucas, C., A. Goeke, R. Briesacher, and R. Bayley. 2007. Phonological Variation in American Sign Language: 2 Hands or 1? Paper presented at NWAV 36, University of Pennsylvania, Philadelphia, October 11–14.

Lucas, C., and C. Valli. 1992. *Language Contact in the American Deaf Community.* San Diego: Academic.

Mauk, C. E., and M. E. Tyrone. 2008. Sign Lowering as Phonetic Reduction in American Sign Language. In R. Sock, S. Fuchs, and Y. Laprie, eds., *International Seminar on Speech Production 2008: Proceedings,* 185–88. Strasbourg: INRIA.

McCaskill, C. 2005. The Education of Black Deaf Americans in the 20th Century: Policy Implications for Administrators in Residential Schools for the Deaf. PhD diss., Gallaudet University.

McKee, D., R. McKee, and G. Major. 2008. Sociolinguistic Variation in NZSL Numerals. In R. M. de Quadros, ed., *Sign Languages: Spinning and Unraveling the Past, Present, and Future: Papers from the 9th Theoretical Issues in Sign Language Research Conference,* 296–313. Petrópolis, RJ, Brazil: Editora Arara Azul.

Mesch, J. 2000. Tactile Swedish Sign Language: Turn-taking in Signed Conversations of People Who Are Deaf and Blind. In M. Metzger, ed., *Bilingualism and Identity in Deaf Communities,* 187–203. Washington, D.C.: Gallaudet University Press.

Metzger, M. 1995. Constructed Dialogue and Constructed Action in American Sign Language. In C. Lucas, ed., *Sociolinguistics in Deaf Communities,* 255–71. Washington, D.C.: Gallaudet University Press.

———. 1999. *Sign Language Interpreting: Deconstructing the Myth of Neutrality.* Washington, D.C.: Gallaudet University Press.

———, and S. Mather. 2004. Constructed Dialogue and Constructed Action in Conversational Narratives in ASL. Poster presented at the Conference on Theoretical Issues in Sign Language Research (TISLR 8), Barcelona, September 30–October 2.

Milroy, L. 1987. *Language and Social Networks,* 2nd ed. Oxford: Blackwell.

Mobley, R. 1991 (February 25). Deaf Teachers of the Deaf. Paper presented at the Conference of the Association of College Educators in Hearing Impairment, Jekyll Island, Ga.

Mufwene, S, J. R. Rickford, G. Bailey, and J. Baugh, eds. 1998. *African-American English.* London: Routledge.

Nadolske, M. A., and R. Rosenstock. 2007. Occurrence of Mouthings in American Sign Language. In P. Perniss, R. Pfau, and M. Steinbach, eds., *Visible Variation: Comparative Studies on Sign Language Structure,* 35–62. Berlin: de Gruyter.

National Black Deaf Advocates. 2002. *Black Deaf Life Stories: An Oral History.* Video. Author.

Neidle, C., J. Kegl, D. MacLaughlin, B. Bahan, and R. G. Lee. 2000. *The Syntax of American Sign Language: Functional Categories and Hierarchical Structure.* Cambridge, Mass.: MIT Press.

Netterville, S. L. 1938. The New State School for Negro Deaf in Louisiana. *American Annals of the Deaf* 83: 448–49.

Neverdon-Morton, C. 1989. *Afro-American Women of the South and the Advancement of the Race, 1895–1925.* Knoxville: University of Tennessee Press.

Ogbu, J. U. 1999. Beyond Language: Ebonics, Proper English, and Identity in a Black-American Speech Community. *American Educational Research Journal* 36: 147–84.

Padden, C., and D. Perlmutter. 1987. American Sign Language and the Architecture of Phonological Theory. *Natural Language and Linguistic Theory* 5: 335–75.

Petronio, K., and D. Lillo-Martin. 1997. WH-movement and the Position of SPEC-CP: Evidence from American Sign Language. *Language* 73: 18–57.

Preston, D. R. 1996. Where the Worst English Is Spoken. In E. W. Schneider, ed., *Focus on the USA,* 297–360. Amsterdam: Benjamins.

Raanes, E. 2006. Å gripe inntrykk og uttrykk: Interaksjon og meningsdanning i døvblindes samtaler. En studie av et utvalg dialoger på taktilt norsk tegnspråk. PhD diss., Sor-Trondelag University College, Norway.

Rainò, P. 2001. Mouthings and Mouth Gestures in Finish Sign Language (FinSL). In P. Boyes Braem and R. Sutton-Spence, eds., *The Hands Are the Head of the Mouth,* 41–50. Hamburg: Signum.

Rayman, J. 1999. Storytelling in the Visual Mode: A Comparison of ASL and English. In E. Winston, ed., *Storytelling and Conversation: Discourse in Deaf Communities,* 59–82. Washington, D.C.: Gallaudet University Press.

Redding, R. 1997. Changing Times, Changing Society: Implications for Professionals in Deaf Education. *American Annals of the Deaf* 142: 83–85.

Rickford, J. R. 1999. *African American Vernacular English: Features, Evolution, Educational Implications.* Oxford: Blackwell.

———, and F. McNair-Knox. 1994. Addressee- and Topic-influenced Style Shift: A Quantitative Sociolinguistic Study. In D. Biber and E. Finegan, eds., *Sociolinguistic Perspectives on Register,* 235–76. New York: Oxford University Press.

Rickford, J. R., and R. J. Rickford. 2000. *Spoken Soul: The Story of Black English.* New York: Wiley.

Riggs, B. M. 1934. *A Brief History of the Education of the Deaf in the State of Arkansas.* Little Rock: Arkansas School for the Deaf.

Ronkin, M., and H. E. Karn. 1999. Mock Ebonics: Linguistic Racism in Parodies of Ebonics on the Internet. *Journal of Sociolinguistics* 3(3): 360–80.

Rosenstock, R. 2003. International Sign: Investigating Its Structure and Use. PhD diss., Gallaudet University.

Roy, C. 1989. Features of Discourse in an American Sign Language Lecture. In C. Lucas, ed., *The Sociolinguistics of the Deaf Community,* 231–51. San Diego: Academic.

Sankoff, D., S. A. Tagliamonte, and E. Smith. 2005. Goldvarb X: A Variable Rule Application for Macintosh and Windows. Computer program. Toronto: Department of Linguistics, University of Toronto.

Schembri, A., and T. Johnston. 2007. Sociolinguistic Variation in the Use of Fingerspelling in Australian Sign Language: A Pilot Study. *Sign Language Studies* 7: 319–47.

———, and D. Goswell. 2006. NAME Dropping: Location Variation in Australian Sign Language. In C. Lucas, ed., *Multilingualism and Sign Languages: From the Great Plains to Australia,* 121–56. Washington, D.C.: Gallaudet University Press.

Schembri, A., D. McKee, R. McKee, S. Pivac, T. Johnstone, and D. Goswell. 2009. Phonological Variation and Change in Australian and New Zealand Sign Languages: The Location Variable. *Language Variation and Change* 21: 193–231.

Schermer, T. 2001. The Role of Mouthings in Sign Language of the Netherlands: Some Implications for the Production of Sign Language Dictionaries. In P. Boyes Braem and R. Sutton-Spence, eds., *The Hands Are the Head of the Mouth,* 273–84. Hamburg: Signum.

Settles, C. J. 1940. Normal Training for Colored Teachers. *American Annals of the Deaf* 85: 209–15.

Skinner, Platt H. 1859. *The Mute and the Blind.* Niagara City, N.Y.: Author.

Smitherman, G. 1977. *Talkin' and Testifyin': The Language of Black America.* Boston: Houghton Mifflin.

Smyrl, V. E. 2001. *The Handbook of Texas Online.* http://www.tsd.state. TX.us.

Stewart, J., K. J. Meier, R. M. LaFollette, and R. E. England. 1989. In Quest of Role Models: Change in Black Teacher Representation in Urban School Districts, 1968–1986. *Journal of Negro Education* 58: 140–52.

Stokoe, W. C., Jr. 1960. *Sign Language Structure: An Outline of Visual Communication Systems of the American Deaf.* Studies in Linguistics: Occasional Paper 8. Buffalo, N.Y.: University of Buffalo Linguistics Department.

———, D. C. Casterline, and C. G. Croneberg. 1965. *A Dictionary of American Sign Language on Linguistic Principles.* Silver Spring, Md.: Gallaudet College Press.

Strömqvist, S., and L. Verhoeven, eds. 2004. *Relating Events in Narrative.* Vol. 2, *Typological and Contextual Perspectives.* Mahwah, N.J.: Erlbaum.

Sutton-Spence, R., and L. Day. 2001. Mouthings and Mouth Gestures in British Sign Language (BSL). In P. Boyes Braem and R. Sutton-Spence, eds., *The Hands Are the Head of the Mouth: The Mouth as Articulator in Sign Languages,* 69–85. Hamburg: Signum.

Tabak, J. 2006. *Significant Gestures: A History of American Sign Language.* Westport, Conn.: Praeger.

Tagliamonte, S. A. 2006. *Analysing Sociolinguistic Variation.* New York: Cambridge University Press.

Tannen, D. 1989. *Talking Voices: Repetition, Dialogue, and Imagery in Conversational Discourse.* New York: Cambridge University Press.

Travis, C. 2007. Genre Effects on Subject Expression in Spanish: Priming in Narrative and Conversation. *Language Variation and Change* 19: 101–33.

Tsl.state.tx.us. Forever Free: The 1870s. Nineteenth-century African-American Legislators and Constitutional Convention Delegates of Texas. A Joint Exhibit from the State Preservation Board and the Texas State Library and Archives Commission.

Vale, J. 1948. Review of Little Paper Family for 1947–1948. *American Annals of the Deaf* 93: 511–62.

Van Cleve, J. V., and B. A. Crouch. 1989. *A Place of Their Own: Creating the Deaf Community in America.* Washington, D.C.: Gallaudet University Press.

Vaughn-Cook, F. A. 2007. Lessons Learned from the Ebonics Controversy: Implications for Language Assessment. In R. Bayley and C. Lucas, eds., *Sociolinguistic Variation: Theories, Methods, and Applications,* 254–75. New York: Cambridge University Press.

Vogt-Svendsen, M. 2001. A Comparison of Mouth Gestures and Mouthings in Norwegian Sign Language (NSL). In P. Boyes Braem and R. Sutton-Spence, eds., *The Hands Are the Head of the Mouth,* 9–40. Hamburg: Signum.

Wait, G. 2008. ASD: The Hartford Connection. Hartford History Center, Hartford Public Library in celebration of Deaf Awareness Week.

Weiler, J. 1990. The School at Allensworth. *Journal of Education* 172: 9–38.

White, S. 1990. Papers on Black Deaf Research Project, MS118 Box 1, Folder 2. Gallaudet University Archives.

Willie, C. V. 1987. The Future of School Desegregation. In J. Dewart, ed., *The State of Black America 1987,* 37–47. New York: National Urban League.

Winford, D. 2003. Ideologies of Language and Socially Realistic Linguistics. In S. Makoni, G. Smitherman, A. F. Ball, and A. K. Spears, eds., *Black Linguistics: Language, Society, and Politics in Africa and the Americas,* 21–30. New York: Routledge.

Wolfram, W. 1991. *Dialects and American English.* Englewood Cliffs, N.J.: Prentice Hall.

———. 1998. Language Ideology and Dialect: Understanding the Oakland Ebonics Controversy. *Journal of English Linguistics* 26: 108–21.

———. 2008. Urban African American Vernacular English: Morphology and Syntax. In E. Schneider, ed., *Varieties of English.* Vol. 2, *The Americas and the Caribbean,* 468–91. Berlin: Mouton de Gruyter.

———, and N. Schilling-Estes. 2006. *American English: Dialects and Variation,* 2nd ed. Oxford: Blackwell.

Wolfram, W., and E. R. Thomas. 2002. *The Development of African American English.* Oxford: Blackwell.

Woll, B. 2001. The Sin That Dares to Speak Its Name: Echo Phonology in British Sign Language (BSL). In P. Boyes Braem and R. Sutton-Spence, eds., *The Hands Are the Head of the Mouth,* 87–98. Hamburg: Signum.

Woodward, J. 1976. Black Southern Signing. *Language in Society* 5: 211–18.

———, and S. DeSantis. 1977. Two to One It Happens: Dynamic Phonology in Two Sign Languages. *Sign Language Studies* 17: 329–46.

———, C. Erting, and S. Oliver. 1976. Facing and Hand(l)ing Variation in American Sign Language. *Sign Language Studies* 10: 43–52.

Wright, M. H. 1999. *Sounds like Home: Growing Up Black and Deaf in the South.* Washington, D.C.: Gallaudet University Press.

Wulf, A., P. Dudis, R. Bayley, and C. Lucas. 2002. Variable Subject Presence in ASL Narratives. *Sign Language Studies* 3: 54–76.

Yates, F. P. 2004. *Brown vs. Board of Education* and Its Impact on Staunton's Virginia School for the Deaf and Blind. Unpublished manuscript, Virginia School for the Deaf and Blind, museum, Staunton, Virginia.

Young, R., and R. Bayley. 1996. VARBRUL Analysis for Second Language Acquisition Research. In R. Bayley and D. R. Preston, eds., *Second Language Acquisition and Linguistic Variation,* 253–306. Amsterdam: Benjamins.

Zeshan, U. 2001. Mouthing in Indopakistani Sign Language (IPSL): Regularities and Variation. In P. Boyes Braem and R. Sutton-Spence, eds., *The Hands Are the Head of the Mouth: The Mouth as Articulator in Sign Languages,* 247–72. Hamburg: Signum.

Index

Figures and tables are indicated with f and t following the page number.